FORGET ME NOT

Frontispiece: Appliqué album quilt, c. 1850, probably Baltimore, Maryland. Maker unknown. 92″ x 91½″. Plain and printed cottons with supplemental inked detail. A splendid floral meander border, fruit and flowers in compotes, eagles, doves, peacocks, and lyres are all part of the usual Baltimore design vocabulary. Two of the city's monuments—the Washington Monument and the Battle Monument—are found occasionally, but the inclusion of the U.S. Capitol and the Baltimore City Hall are rare achievements. This was probably a presentation quilt; one wonders whether the recipient had strong political aspirations.

FORGET ME NOT

A GALLERY OF FRIENDSHIP AND ALBUM QUILTS

by Jane Bentley Kolter

THE MAIN STREET PRESS • PITTSTOWN, NEW JERSEY

This book is dedicated to my husband, Edward O'Brien, and sons, Matthew and Winfield, for all their patience and help. In the words of one woman who signed an album quilt "Mary April 4th 1854":

In the hours of calm reflection
In the hours of special glee
If thou shouldst in recollection
Think of any, think of me.

First edition 1985

All rights reserved

Copyright © 1985 by Jane Bentley Kolter

Published by
The Main Street Press, Inc.
William Case House
Pittstown, NJ 08867

Published simultaneously in Canada by
Methuen Publications
2330 Midland Avenue
Agincourt, Ontario M1S 1P7

Printed in the United States of America

Library of Congress Cataloging in Publication Data

Kolter, Jane Bentley.
   Forget me not.
   Bibliography, p. 127.
   1. Quilting—United States—History. 2. Coverlets—
United States—History. I. Title.
TT835.K65   1985   746.9'7'0973   85-7309
ISBN 0-915590-68-9
ISBN 0-915590-67-0 (pbk.)

 # Contents

Preface

American quilts have always been an intriguing subject, for me and for thousands of others. Album and friendship quilts hold a special fascination. Each makes a clear statement about the women who fashioned it, because each album or friendship quilt holds the makers' *own* words, signatures, and some particular patterned remembrance. After all, the first function of an album or friendship quilt is remembrance—a usable memorial filled with personal statements.

Face to face with these memorials for forgotten people, I found the textiles, needlework, and design so compelling that I became engrossed in puzzling out each square, signature, and inscription. I often found myself thinking of Dr. William Rush Dunton's observation on seeing his first album—that he had "met" an interesting quilt.

Photographs in books rarely show the "real" quilt. If a whole quilt is pictured, the photograph can't show tiny inscriptions or fine stitches in appliqué or embroidered motifs. Nor can a photograph detail the bad things that happen to old quilts. Sometimes, no matter what care has been lavished on a bed cover, blocks contain deteriorating fabrics, places where dyes have actually eaten through the material, leaving neat holes where black or yellow once appeared. Whenever possible in this book, particularly interesting inscriptions are transcribed and embroidered details mentioned, but I have not pointed out the sad, but inevitable, deterioration which is occasionally present.

The captions and text follow certain conventions. If I call a bed cover a "quilt," it contains stuffing. Crazy patchwork throws, however, are an exception. Even dictionaries call these unstuffed pieces "quilts." I use the word "coverlet" rather than the term "summer spread" to indicate an unstuffed pieced or appliqué bed cover. The phrase "summer spread" is not listed in period literature which I have seen, and I suspect it was coined much later.

Caption format is fairly standard. First to appear is a summary of fabrication techniques and quilt purpose, if known. Dates follow: "c." (circa) is an estimate and "d." means there is a specific date inscribed on the quilt itself. I have included as much information as possible on quilt origins. The phrase "maker unknown" is generic—certainly many quilts had more than one seamstress at work. If a piece is obviously the work of a single woman, I have tried to mention it in the caption text and give the reasons. Length precedes width in every case where measurements are given. (If these are omitted, the data is currently unavailable.) Textiles are listed in the approximate order of amounts used in a piece.

Throughout the text, the first mention of a new term common to an earlier parlance is usually enclosed in quotation marks. All material in quotation marks is verbatim, and spellings are taken directly from the source.

Studying old friendship quilts has given me the opportunity to make and renew my own friendships with colleagues, collectors, and dealers working on quilt history. I would like to thank especially Patricia T. Herr and Sabra Petersman, Gloria Seaman Allen, Neill Allen, Inez Brooks-Meyers, Ann Barton Brown, Ruth Hagy, Susan Anderson Haye, Catherine Jansen, Joan Johnson, A. Bruce MacLeish, Jaime Matouch, Marsha McDowell, Celia Oliver, Sterling Rayburn, Robin S. Roberts, Susan Rousseau, Stella Rubin, Jackie Schneider, Jean Severa, Ludy Strauss, Lotus Stack, Jean Svedlenak, Ross Trump, and Shelly Zegart, each of whom has been very helpful. I am also most grateful to Charles Bolton, Jim Clokey, Ann Coleman, Judith Coram, Margaret DiSalvi, Kathryn V. Dixson, Ray Featherstone, Mr. and Mrs. Herbert Feldman, Amy Finkel, Laura Fisher, Sandi Fox, Barbara Franco, Eleanor Gustafson, Phyllis Haders, Viola Holmes, Kay Hudek, Dena Katzenberg, Rod Lich, Sandra Mitchell, Bettie Mintz, Pat Nikols, Susan Parrett, Nancy Pearson, Bets Ramsey, Merry Silber, and Anne Watkins for their important contributions.

Museums, private collectors, and dealers in American quilts have contributed a great deal to this book. I particularly want to thank staff members of the following museums: The Abby Aldrich Rockefeller Folk Art Center, The Atlanta Historical Society, The Allen County Historical Society, The Brooklyn Museum, Chester County Historical Society, The Daughters of the American Revolution Museum, Collections of Greenfield Village and the Henry Ford Museum, Independence National Historical Park, The Kansas City Museum, Maryland Historical Society, Museum of Our National Heritage, Folk Arts Division—The Michigan State University Museum, New York State Historical Association, The Newark Museum, The Oakland Museum, Philadelphia Museum of Art, The Shelburne Museum, The Sloan Museum, The Smithsonian Institute, Southern Oregon Historical Society, State Historical Society of Wisconsin, and The Wadsworth Athenaeum. Dorothy Brooks, David Cunningham, Marston Luce, Pink House Antiques, and Tewksbury Antiques also helped considerably.

To name all of the curators, quilt dealers, and collectors who were unstintingly helpful would be impossible. All of them have a love of their collections and dedication which just seems to make them naturally want to help. Finally, this book would have been impossible without the assistance of Frank Mahood, Lawrence Grow, and Martin Greif and the inspiration of William Cobbett.

Introduction

ALBUM and friendship quilts share a common history with other American quilted coverlets; perhaps they also have more history. Every quilt is intimately tied to its maker. Every woman who made or worked on any quilt left something of herself in the stitches. But in album and friendship quilts, women tried to make their intentions explicit.

Friendship quilts were often the best bedcover a family owned. They were made for an event, a person, or some special purpose which set them apart from everyday life and, so, were more important than the utility quilts which ordinarily dressed a bed. The everyday coverlet has rarely survived the rough use of several generations. Album and friendship quilts, on the other hand, were treasured tokens, carefully preserved. Owning one became a responsibility to pay attention to the makers' requests of "Forget Me Not" or "Remember Me."

Here are textile reflections of a sudden growth of sentiment or, more truthfully, the self-conscious sentimentality which played a large role in the lives of American women in the mid-19th century. The term they chose for such feeling was *sensibility*, and everyone could admit to knowing one or two friends with an excess of sensibility. Perhaps this was one response to the great religious awakening sweeping the country. However it came about, romantic imagery and expansive patriotism replaced the more austere classical ideals of the new republic.

This lively period (1810-1840) encouraged a number of remembrances, beginning with the mourning art and needlework of the early 19th century. And books known as "annuals," also advertised as "albums," were sold from the end of the 1820s, particularly as New Year's presents. What better gift, after all, than a record for the upcoming year? A particularly nice example of an album, now in the collections of the Henry Francis Du Pont Winterthur Museum, was compiled by Mary Bachman of Charlestown, South Carolina, between 1833 and 1836. The title page is engraved "Album," enclosed in a flourished cartouche. On the second page, Mary inked: "The Friendly Repository/AND KEEPSAKE/of/MARY ELIZA BACHMAN/1835." Over the years, her friends added many couplets, quotations, drawings, and good wishes. Such small tokens of sentiment may have inspired women to create in fabric some useful display of their artistry and affection. So they worked coverlets which could combine the necessary needlework skills demanded of their sex with sentiments they cherished. These quilts were literally album books in cloth.

Album and friendship quilts began to appear in numbers about 1840. Both were made up of blocks. While the friendship quilt might be fashioned in one of the traditional pieced or appliqué patterns, the album quilt was not. Like the scrapbooks and friendly repositories of the day, album quilts had something very much like pages—each square was different and each carried a signature in the way it was worked. Some even had inscriptions in the block or a name or initial added in cross-stitch embroidery. These album quilts were initially a refinement of the appliqué chintz coverlet combined with squares of the better-known appliqué and pieced patterns.

Even though most friendship and album quilts are made in blocks, important exceptions exist. Work might be done by one or more seamstresses in appliqué, or laid-on, work. Piecework—the joining of pre-cut patches—or a combination of appliqué and piecework might be used. When only one maker was involved, the quilt could be more of a sampler or display of patterns. Botanical albums and some of the other pieced and crazy quilts fall into this category.

When entire quilts or the individual squares are signed by their makers, they provide modern students, geneologists, and collectors with a chance for a research field day. Sometimes, one or two women with particularly fine handwriting added all of the names on squares intended for inclusion in a single quilt. If there were many friends contributing to a presentation quilt, these spreads could be huge, and deciphering them a real challenge. Fortunately, one individual was usually the supervisor of assembling the blocks, but album design could and did get out of hand in some cases. Whether these look a little "folksy" or just plain disorganized is sometimes a matter of luck.

Album quilts were first made in a relatively small geographic area focused on Pennsylvania and Maryland, but the idea spread rapidly along the settlement pattern lines appearing in the growing country. Within a decade, they were made in middle New York, and techniques and designs followed women who moved into the Western Reserve area of Ohio. Many Pennsylvanians traveled straight westward, through Lancaster County and into central Ohio and Indiana. So did their quilts and their patterns. Other Pennsylvania Germans, especially Moravians, migrated southward through Maryland and the Valley of Virginia. Their patterns appear as far south as the Winston-Salem and New Bern areas in North Carolina. Baltimore, between 1846 and 1852, was the undisputed center of fine album quiltmaking, but other areas developed their own interpretations of the style. Some of the illustrations in this book should help to define these trends.

Earlier bedcoverings contributed to the design development of the album. Palampores, for instance, were one important antecedent of certain pieces. We still see palampores today as the Indian bedspreads of college dormitories and first apartments. Eighteenth-century pieces were finer—the dyes were more brilliant; patterns were more complex; and the printing was often perfectly executed. But they were still one-piece Indian spreads. When first imported to England in the 17th century, palampores were curiosities but not really desirable. So importers tried to make them more saleable by bringing English designs back to the East for copying on new spreads. These suc-

1. One-piece friendship quilt, d. 1761, Pennsylvania, Philadelphia area. Drawn by Sarah Smith and stitched by Hannah Callendar and Catherine Smith. 94¾" x 96". Silk face, printed cotton back. The design stitched on this rare quilt is a variant of one made in the Philadelphia Quaker community at the time. This is the only one of the six or seven coverlets in the group which is signed and dated. The central medallion features a pastoral scene with two animals that might be cows.

ceeded so well that the "chints," as palampores and other multicolored Indian cottons were also called, remained popular throughout the 18th century.

Europeans could not equal the brilliant colors, stable dyes, and the exotic imagery which guaranteed the appeal of Indian cottons. Most dyes everywhere were derived from plants like indigo and madder. These were set by applying appropriate mordant, or mineral solution, to the piece to be dyed. (Urine and dung were common mordants, so dye works were not always the most pleasant of places.) Mordants were mixed in a paste and applied to the fabrics with wooden blocks, just as wood-block prints are done. They might also be applied freehand, a technique called "penciling." The entire cloth was then put into a boiling dye bath and left for an appropriate amount of time. Areas which were to remain white were painted over with wax before the piece was immersed. Eastern textile "painters" had simply mastered more of the chemical and printing process. Their work was so much in demand that laws were passed in England prohibiting the use and wearing of chintz and calico.

Entire palampores are occasionally found as the top layer of "whole-cloth" quilts, and some of these are among the earliest surviving American pieces. Imported chintz also animated English and, later, American textile printers. Indian designs, especially the Tree of Life, were copied by needleworkers on both sides of the Atlantic. And, finally, when worn beyond any hope of repair, palampores and calicos provided hundreds of scraps that could be cut and pieced or appliquéd to make new and original coverlet tops. Some of these were used as simple spreads; others were backed, filled with batting, and quilted.

Women also dressed their petticoats with decorative quilting, adding both texture and warmth. Silk and glazed textiles, like calimanco (often miscalled lindsey-woolsey), were favored. Their sheen was enhanced by lines of quilting. Along with white marseilles, another petticoat favorite, these textiles were chosen for tops of quilted coverlets. This is another type of one-piece coverlet—one which depended on the stitched pattern for its interest. The patterns were often bold combinations of conventionalized flowers, leaves, and feathers standing out in high relief against the plain ground. These same motifs are found as appliquéd cutout designs on the quilts of the 1840s, appearing in many of the album and friendship quilts. But the designs did not appear in a vacuum—they had long been a part of things women saw every day. Even a woman who could not read could appreciate some of the printers' ornaments found on broadsides and books. Or she might find some motif on a transfer-printed plate, carved or inlaid in a piece of furniture, or on a printed textile.

The earliest friendship quilt illustrated in this book (fig. 1) is a beautifully wrought one-piece spread with a top of light-blue silk. Three young Quaker women worked on the spread and quilted their inscription in tiny running stitch along the top edge: "Drawn by Sarah Smith Sti[t]ched by Hannah Callendar and Catherine Smith in Testimony of their Friendship 10 mo 5th 1761." Early signed quilts and other needlework done by Friends, as Quakers are more properly styled, often feature the plain numerical designations for months and days of the week. It was only as Friends became more worldly that the common English terms were used.

In the 19th-century album quilt, women often used a printed appliqué piece on a plain ground. Appliqué chintz spreads were one of these types. For these bedcovers, attractive chintz motifs were carefully cut from their ground and sewn on a different backing. Initially, these were probably salvage operations—clever ways to preserve well-loved Indian palampores and chintzes. Quilted spreads of this type began to appear in the mid-18th century. The first documented appliqué chintz *friendship* coverlet is the unquilted example made on the adjoining Westover-Berkley plantations of Virginia (see fig. 208, Safford and Bishop, *America's Quilts and Coverlets*). Chintz appliqué of this

2. Piecework and appliqué marriage quilt, d. 1785, Maine. 86" x 81". Cotton and wool. Appliqué inscription reads, "Anna Tuels her bed quilt given to her by her mother in the year Au 23 1785," and is spaced around the four hearts appearing at the corners of the center square. Combinations of piecework and appliqué show up frequently in early album and friendship quilts and again in the crazy quilt genre. The pieced blocks are rarely the same, as they are here. In this quilt the piecing represents a veritable sampler of late-18th-century printed and woven textiles.

3. Appliqué remembrance quilt, d. 1846, Pennsylvania, Pottstown area. Made by Esther J. White and signed by several family members. 105" x 104". Printed cottons; ink inscriptions. Esther White has taken a number of designs often used in appliqué quilts and combined them in this open, balanced quilt which is not wholly typical of Pennsylvania examples of the period.

sort created new pictures from cut motifs, often recreating a Tree of Life or vase of flowers. In the late 19th century the technique was dubbed "Broderie Perse," most likely in an editorial search for new names for old, a favorite Victorian pastime.

Piecework quilts were probably made at the same time that one-piece quilts were being fashioned. This piecing technique is often called "patchwork," though that term more suits appliqué techniques. Because pieced quilts were constructed of small bits of fabric sewn together, and because most were subjected to heavier use than the show quilts were, few early examples survive. Early albums often have a few piecework squares mixed with the more usual appliqué. And, by about 1850, one piecework pattern, the Chimney Sweep, had become a universal favorite for the autograph quilt.

If all of these needlework techniques can be used to make album or friendship quilts, what exactly are they? Think of them as the quilts of sentiment and remembrance, pieces well-defined by a verse—a common variant of one stitched on samplers of earlier centuries and fortuitously inked on a quilt:

> This quilt behind me I will leave —
> When I am in my silent grave.
> That my dear friends may view it o'er
> And think of me when I'm no more.
>
> 1846   By Esther J. White

4. Signature block of Esther White's quilt, fig. 3. This touching message has lost none of its poignancy for all the use it has had on samplers, on tombstones, and on quilts.

The verse begs no questions about the maker's purpose in the creation of her work. Esther White sought and has achieved a degree of immortality beyond the compass of her days.

Most album and friendship quilts were made for other reasons. These might be some sort of commemoration—perhaps only the joy of shared techniques or, as Dr. William Rush Dunton suggests in *Old Quilts*, a spirit of competition. But they are always quilts with a purpose. In *Quilts in America*, Patsy and Myron Orlovsky say of this genre that "Most special quilts are distinguished in the same way that a wedding cake is distinguished from a normal one—the materials are the same, the techniques are the same, but the intentions are different. They were made for special reasons. . . ." Who could put it better than that?

Quilt lovers have been giving names to the several sorts of special quilts for nearly a century. Among these quilts, the Orlovskys identify various types of sampler quilts, memory quilts, mourning, and commemorative quilts. The commemorative pieces particularly show patriotic themes, political and social events. Other types include brides' quilts, presentation, friendship, friendship medley, freedom, and autograph quilts. In addition, Bible quilts that quote Scripture passages were made, and subscription quilts flourished from the last quarter of the 19th century until about 1930. Examples of all of these types will be shown in the pages following.

5. Detail of fig. 3.

FORGET ME NOT

1. "Gaiety of Dress": The Appliqué Chintz Quilt and Coverlet

INDIAN chintz proved fascinating from its first European introduction in the 17th century. This cotton textile—printed with floral designs, glowing but subtle colors, and intricate patterns—is still in demand today. Imagine how coveted it was at a time when fabrics with small, closely repeated red, blue, or brown flowers, or some other tiny pattern, were all that English and European textile printers could produce! Chintz— or occasionally calico, another cotton—was worked into seat covers, bed furniture, and even dresses and other clothing. Its competition was so severe that English woolen and silk workers successfully petitioned Parliament to forbid its use and kept out some imports and local cotton printing between 1700 and about 1775. But these cottons were made into coverlets and worn on the streets in defiance of all prohibition, and chintz never lost its grip upon women of the 18th century. Its use in bed covers began with the first imported palampore, and continued in appliqué chintz spreads of the first two thirds of the 19th century. There are even chintz spreads being manufactured today.

Chintz and calico can be generally characterized as all-cotton cloth. While calico might be quite plain, having striped or checked weave in white or colors, the chintz was —as its Hindi derivitive suggests—variegated. Not only variegated, but often brilliantly colored and usually glazed to add to its vibrancy, chintz was well-suited to furnishings. Its slick surface repelled a certain amount of dirt and wear. Calico more often served as a dress fabric. Both were used in bed covers.

The English were producing furnishing chintzes which nearly equaled Indian cottons by the time of the American Revolution. As soon as trade was resumed, these textiles were exported in quantity. Shortly after the Revolution, American block-printers, like John Hewson of Philadelphia, also succeeded in printing furnishing cottons to grace the bed.

By the end of the 18th century, chintz furnishing fabrics were being made in small panels used for chair seats and backs. These were often used with other printed panels and borders, put together like jigsaw puzzles, with chintz medallions as the center-

6. *Opposite page:* Appliqué chintz crib quilt, d. 1847, American. 47" x 33". Inscribed in stem stitch in center block, "To Mary E. Price from her mother/ 1847." Printed chintz and plain cotton. Although appliqué chintz, or Broderie Perse, was a favored technique in the mid-Atlantic and southern states, examples in a crib size are rare. It is difficult to imagine a more touching sort of presentation than this.

pieces in larger designs. Wallpapers, too, were printed with special medallions and borders which could be cut and applied separately or of-a-piece, as the user desired. Thomas Sheraton, the noted English designer, even specified chairs with set-in panels: "The figures in the tablet above the front rail are of French printed silk or satin sewed on the stuffing with borders round them. The seat and the back are of the same kind. . . ." Cotton and linen printers never lingered far behind those working on finer textiles.

In the late 18th century and early 19th century, cutout chintz motifs were frequently used in appliqué on marseilles and lighter plain-weave grounds. By the end of the second decade of the 19th century, this fashion had assumed the proportions of a fad in coverlets. Sometimes pirated motifs were cut and applied wholesale to their ground, but, as the fad gathered converts, a flower or leaf was cut from one cotton furnishing cloth and combined with other elements cut from the same or from a different fabric altogether. Entire designs were worked out for a whole-cloth spread, and the chintz cut and sewed on to meet the pattern. But, for friendship albums, blocks were individually prepared. These were later set together with or without printed bands, called sashes, to separate the squares. Some added borders to complement the blocks, and very particular needlewomen might give friends the chintzes to cut so that everything might work well together and the design be unified.

The blocks for the top might be of one size, or smaller squares might combine with a larger center block or blocks. All might be signed, and a few squares include dates, verses, and little sketches. Large blocks quite naturally carried the most important messages—often a dedication or particular remembrance. How poignant some were! For instance, in the central row of fig. 9, the names "Thomas Watson" and "Mary B. Watson" are inscribed along with this verse:

> Our love has been no common love
> With hopeful smiles and tears:
> Our faith is faith to meet above,
> Our trust is trust of years.

> And being one through life's long day,
> Where faith so oft hath striven,
> When love no more shall weep and pray,
> We must be one in heaven.

The combinations of chintz motifs and coverlet designs were many and varied, but this fashion seems to have been relatively limited. Most coverlets of appliqué chintz produced after about 1835 come from mid-Atlantic and southern states. Those from the Deep South are often unquilted spreads, as a warmer climate really did not encourage investment in quilted bed covers. Although appliqué chintz spreads continued to be made until just before the Civil War, they were superseded in most areas by the colorful album quilt.

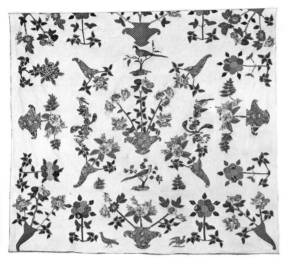

7. *Above:* Appliqué counterpane, early 19th century, American, possibly New England. Maker unknown. 100" x 100". Chintz and other printed cottons. This spread has some design similarity to the Indian palampores. Straight, thin stems and sparse appliqué suggest a New England origin.

8. *Top right:* Appliqué quilt top, c. 1830, possibly New Jersey or Pennsylvania. Attrib. Hannah Stockton. 105" x 92". Chintz and other printed cottons. A late revival of the Tree of Life is bordered with vignettes of shipping trades and daily life. Two figures at the bottom corners are cut from an indigo block-print of the 18th century. The village scenes include a tavern, with hanging sign, and a woman returning from milking with two buckets of milk.

9. *Right:* Appliqué chintz memorial quilt, d. 1846, 1847, American; Pennsylvania and Maryland noted. 98" x 104". Printed chintz and plain cottons. This memorial and friendship quilt was evidently the work of a widespread group of friends. Inscriptions are in varied hands, and most in the central squares concern the Ricketts and Watson families.

10. Detail of center square of the Moore friendship quilt, fig. 11.

11. Appliqué chintz friendship quilt, dedicated in center block: "Aunt Eliza Moore/Trenton, N.J./March 4th, 1843." Made by Emma Maria Fish. 101" x 104". Printed chintz and plain cottons. This impressive friendship album was signed by members of the Moore, Fish, Howell and Stryker families and their friends in the Trenton, Philadelphia, Princeton, and Pennington area. The individual blocks are dated between November, 1842, and January 31, 1844. Emma Maria Fish signed the back of the quilt. A number of hands added the inscriptions.

12. Appliqué cotton print friendship block, d. 1848, probably Placerville, California. 10" x 10". Made by or for Mrs. Jane L. Ayres. The furnishing print with charming chinoiserie figures is similar in design to copperplate-printed textiles of the last quarter of the 18th century, though it is printed as other chintzes were. If this quilt block did come from the gold fields, as its history relates, one can only imagine the life of Mrs. Ayres at the time and what sort of reminiscences the cheerful print must have recalled.

13. Detail of an appliqué chintz friendship quilt, c. 1845-1855. Pennsylvania, Philadelphia area. Made for or by Margaret Donaldson Boggs. 104" x 126". Printed chintz, toile and plain cottons. This quilt belonged to Margaret Donaldson Boggs, a niece of Elizabeth Griscom, who is better known today as Betsy Ross. Most squares of the huge spread are traditional cut and appliqué floral chintz elements, but this charming block features an announcing angel and a palm tree, both cut from earlier textiles. Why this single block was added and what it represented will always be a puzzle.

14. Appliqué chintz quilt, c. 1850-1860, Georgia. Liberty County. Made by a member of the Rev. Dr. Charles Colcock Jones family, Montevideo Plantation. 92½″ x 91¾″. Printed chintz and plain cottons. Family letters may have referred to the fine chintz spread in 1862. This botanical album could hardly escape notice with its familiar and exotic chintz blossoms, separated by brilliant red sashes and bordered in another red print.

15. Appliqué chintz presentation coverlet, unfinished, d. 1850, 1854, 1855, Southern United States. Maker unknown. 109″ x 112″. Inscribed in ink: "To my mother/ 1854", "Sister Polly from Mary/ 1850", and "To my cousin Mary from R.I.W./ 1850", among others. Printed chintz and plain cottons. Local history has it that during the Civil War the quilt was carried from its southern home by a New Hampshire soldier.

16. Appliqué chintz friendship quilt, mid-19th century, Frederick, Maryland. Designed by Mrs. Francis Montague Montell (Johanna Penelope Elizabeth Cushing, 1784-1857). 102" x 101¼". Printed chintz and plain cottons. The friends and family of Mrs. Montell gave the appliquéd chintz blocks. Some are signed: "Grandma Montell", "Mrs. Sterling", "Eliza Montell", "Emily Wildgoss", and "Matilda F. Blair". It is easy to see the beginning of a new album vocabulary in this splendid diagonal-set quilt.

17. Appliqué album quilt, c. 1845, probably Maryland. Maker unknown. 104″ x 111″. Printed chintz, figured and plain cottons.

There are no inscriptions or marks on this transitional quilt to give a clue to its maker. Here is a combination of the techniques of chintz appliqué with squares in the more conventional style. Wreaths, crossed laurels and oak leaves, along with the cutwork squares point to a Maryland origin.

2. "Remember Me": The Album Appliqué Quilt and Coverlet

The very term *album quilt* suggests variety. These appliqué coverlets are usually composed of from sixteen to thirty-six squares, each different and often wildly imaginative. In fact, in *Old Quilts* Dr. William Rush Dunton has called these the "wild" quilts, or "those in which the maker's fancy for design was untrammeled by convention and she executed something varying from the beautiful to the grotesque, but usually original." He goes on to say that the "tame or domesticated quilts . . . are those which follow a conventional pattern and all of the blocks are similar in design."

Most of the quilts in this tradition are what might be called the large-square albums. Blocks in these pieces are appliquéd and range in size from unseamed dimensions of nearly eighteen inches to twelve inches at the smallest. Another group of coverlets, made in New York and New Jersey, features a smaller block which does not exceed eleven inches on a side before it is seamed. In *America's Quilts and Coverlets* Safford and Bishop have drawn an interesting comparison between small-square, crewel-worked coverlets and the earthenware tiles so favored in the homes of Dutch settlers in those areas. The same comparison might apply equally to appliquéd small-square spreads. They come from a Dutch-inspired design vocabulary. A few examples of this type of album coverlet are shown later in this chapter.

Common to most of these spreads are the patterns now considered the mainstay of traditional appliqué vocabulary. These designs form the basis of many single-motif quilts. Geometric patterns are often seen in albums, spaced among the unique squares. Star and hexagonal mosaic and other conventional patterns, like the Wild Goose Chase, are sometimes found. Other blocks feature natural elements. Among these are the leaf patterns—particularly the crossed laurel, oak, and palm. All derived from a shared iconography of honor and enduring strength and were particularly suited to albums presented to some especially worthy, and fortunate, member of the community. Other favorites are the abstract fleur-de-lis, a different type of crossed fleuron which resembles a pomegranate or pineapple, and a number of unique cutwork designs that are part of a long-standing tradition of decorative paper cutting. The cutwork designs were particular favorites among German women who had emigrated to America. Some of these appliqué blocks have patterns which are so finely cut that the fabric is only an eighth of an inch thick when sewn.

18. Pieced and appliqué album presentation quilt, d. 1843-1846, Virginia and Maryland. Apparently made for Agnes Luman. 112" x 100". Printed and plain cottons. Recorded in the center block is Agnes Luman's name and the date of the quilting—September, 1846. Each of the thirty squares features a different bold appliqué in roller-printed fabrics, and most are signed by friends living in Baltimore and Frederick County, Maryland, and Jefferson and Augusta County, Virginia. Nearly every block contains a passage from Psalms or a Wesley hymn, indicating a strong tie with the Methodist Church. Both men and women have signed the quilt.

19. Detail of fig. 18.

20. Appliqué album quilt, d. 1846, 1847, Baltimore, Maryland. 115″ x 115″. Printed and plain cottons; silk embroidery and ink inscriptions. This marvelous early Baltimore album quilt has a number of unusual cutwork blocks among the other foliage and wreath designs. A silhouetted dog, seen upside-down in the upper right-hand corner, is particularly personal and a very rare detail. Among the ink inscriptions are: "Mrs. M. Tydings; M.A. Alden/ 1846 [signed three squares]; Oliv[?]ia Eloise/ Mr. Busty/ Elizabeth George/ Baltimore, Md.; Mary E. Harrison/ 1846 [who signed two squares]; May 16, 1846; W. Chase/ 1847 [twice]; Mary I. Chase/ 1847; Alinerva; T. J. Gorsoch [twice]; Sister Eliza; Mother; Leonora B. Parks [twice]; Sarah A. Pawley/ 1846; Elizabeth A. Searley; Sarah B. Cook; and Julia Ann Young [each twice]". Brilliant chintz borders and sashes unify the diagonal-set quilt.

C. M. Chamberlain

21. *Above:* Pieced and appliqué album quilt, d. 1844, Maryland. Center cross-stitched: "Sarah A. White/ November/1844." 102½" x 119". Printed and plain cottons, linen backing. Several blocks carry cross-stitch initials, while C. M. Chamberlain and E. A. Sabel stitched their full names. Perhaps the ambitious size of the spread exceeded the skills of those contributing to the album.

22. *Left:* Detail of fig. 21. The bird in this square closely resembles Audubon's passenger pigeon.

Flowers, Wreaths, and Baskets

Wreaths are another mark of tribute which frequently appears on album quilts. Some were textile interpretations of the laurel wreath, a signal honor from time immemorial. Floral wreaths, too, were for special occasions in public life—marriages, consecrations, and other more social events. Their appearance on album quilts often announces some analogous activity in the life of a quilt's recipient, but this isn't always the case. As the design vocabulary became more established, wreaths were probably included because they looked good and broke up the format of squares. Some of the most attractive wreaths have clusters of fruit, often grapes or cherries. Heart-shaped garlands, on the other hand, usually did indicate that a wedding was being celebrated. Broken wreaths often enclosed some important figure, and single crossed sprays of foliage were another common quilt element of this type.

Flowers and flowers in baskets and other containers have always been given as gifts for special occasions—and sometimes for no occasion at all. It seems very appropriate to include them on the album quilt. They appeared in profusion. In a few blocks, the appliqué design was

23. Appliqué botanical album quilt, c. 1850, Maryland, Baltimore area. Made by Cinthia Arsworth. 92″ x 80¼″. Printed and plain cottons. An unusual meander border frames the large center square with its basket of fruit, flowers, and bold foliage. Clever use of rainbow and woodgrain prints adds dimension to leaves, fruit, and flowers throughout the quilt, ranking it among the finest of the classical Baltimore pieces. It is not, however, typical of the genre.

adapted almost directly from an element found on printed furnishing chintz, but it was made up of individual scraps of fabric carefully cut and applied to recreate the printed original. Bouquets may be simple or quite complex.

Containers like vases and pots reflect the trends of the ceramic and glass industries at the time. And baskets, particularly, display the quilt maker's virtuosity. In a Baltimore quilt, the woven reeds and wicker might be indicated by using a rainbow print fabric, or they might be cut as individual strips and laid down, then intertwined before actually being sewn to the quilt square. Sometimes these vases and baskets were stuffed with extra filling through the back of the block, giving them an added dimension on the finished quilt. In fact, the extra stuffing—now called trapunto—was an important feature in classical album quilts.

Flowers, of course, had their own language, and the recipients of the quilt could easily read a message contained in a bouquet. About 1818, *La Langage des Fleurs* was published under the pseudonym of "Charlotte de la Tour." This book was often copied, plagiarized and revised—correctly and incorrectly. Sadly, the original meanings were written and rewritten in the Victorian period, and much of the original intent is clouded today. Some meanings can still be deciphered. Red roses, for instance, have long been a symbol for romantic love. White lilies,

24. Appliqué album quilt, d. 1850, 1854, Maryland, Montgomery County. Made by Mary E. Mannakee (c. 1827-?). 99½" x 99½ ". Printed and plain cottons, with gold thread embroidery. Three ink inscriptions have been added in individual squares: "Miss Mary E. Mannakee/ Sept. 20th 1850", "M E Mannakee/ 1850/ Sept.", and "Mary, remember me/ William Thomas Johnson/ 1854". Because the fabric, design, and workmanship of this quilt are so consistent, it is likely that Miss Mannakee was the only seamstress involved in making it. It is less boldly graphic than a classic Baltimore album, featuring a number of cut paper designs and thinly cut foliage motifs. The border is very sparse and attenuated.

sacred to the Virgin Mary for centuries, stand for purity. Yellow tulips say "hopeless love"; blue violets speak of faithfulness; and sweet violets signify modesty. In quilt squares with bouquets and wreaths, the flower-by-flower analysis might turn up surprising meanings.

Fruit was another favored album motif. Baskets and epergnes—a footed dish—often held graceful mounds of melons, apples, pears, and grapes. When displayed in paired cornucopias filled with fruits and flowers, the suggestion was clearly one of peace and plenty. Many authors have commented upon the connection of these fruit-filled containers with the theorem stencil— work done on velvets and other textiles. In Baltimore quilts, the fruit achieved a high degree of naturalism. Dena Katzenberg, in her unparalled catalogue, *Baltimore Album Quilts,* mentions how individual printed fabrics could be used to great effect in achieving such results. As an example, she mentions that "ripple printed rainbow cloth made realistic melon rinds and fruit skins," and goes on to show how Baltimore women used this same fabric for "reflections of water on a rowboat, windblown leaves, stems and foliage, flower petals, and surface undulations on compotes and vases." But Baltimore quilts were remarkable in their use of varied fabrics. Most needlewomen chose a small all-over dress print to achieve their design.

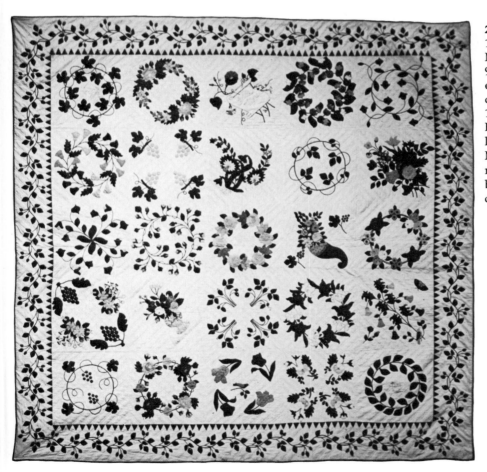

25. Appliqué album bridal quilt, d. 1851, Carroll County, Maryland. Made by Elizabeth Jane Baile. 92" x 92". Printed and plain cottons, silk embroidery. Ink inscription on the quilt reads: "Commenced June 1850"/ "Finished Oct. 30. 1851." Elizabeth Jane Baile made this lovely tribute to her fiancé, Levi Manahan, before they were married on October 30, 1851. Wreaths, bouquets, and an inscribed poem commemorate the occasion.

26. Appliqué album quilt, c. 1850, Maryland. Maker unknown. 102¼" x 105⅝". Printed and plain cottons, velvet; wool and silk embroidery; ink details and inscriptions. Pieced stepped-block outer and inner borders surround splendid green swags and red bowknots. Nine center squares contain patriotic and personal messages—the eagle, Baltimore's Washington Monument, a sailor, and a sturdy couple, perhaps betrothed. Four insets of initials are worked on various squares.

27. Appliqué album quilt, mid-19th century, Baltimore, Maryland. Made by Rachel Meyer (1818-1867). 99½" x 143". Printed and plain cotton and linen. A large center square, reminiscent of a palampore design, is set off with sashing. Mounted cavaliers ride beneath the sparse central floral arrangement. Other squares feature fish and animals. The squirrel in his wreath, a horse and two reindeer somewhat incongrously standing beneath a flower arrangement, add to the charm of this quilt. Its scalloped meander border is rare, and expertly worked.

28. Appliqué album quilt, c. 1850[?], Baltimore, Maryland. Wreaths; flowers in sprays, baskets, and vases; and flocks of birds surround an unusual center square. On a log cabin, with a flag and hard cider barrel to proclaim the maker's support of the 1840 Whig candidate, William Henry Harrison, perch a mysterious rooster and racoon—symbols whose meaning has been lost.

29. Appliqué album quilt top, unfinished, c. 1850, probably Maryland. 98" x 98". Plain and printed cottons with wool embroidery. A strong festoon border, broken with bowknots and tassels, adds to the bold designs of individual blocks. This appears to be the work of a single maker, but she has left no inscriptions to record her identity or her reasons for making the quilt top.

Other Symbols, Sashes, and Borders

The meaning of many emblematic motifs on album quilts, like the language of flowers, has been lost or may have been too personal to have been recorded. The books of emblems which were published and republished from the time when books were first printed disappeared from the common press and could only be found in museums and libraries by the end of the

30. *Opposite page:* Appliqué album presentation quilt, c. 1850, Baltimore, Maryland. Maker unknown. 89″ x 89″. Printed and plain cottons. Doves and hearts suggest a marriage celebration. An unusual oak-leaf border encloses floral and Odd Fellows squares. Rainbow fabrics in flowers and in the eagle confirm a Baltimore origin.

31. *Right:* Detail of eagle in fig. 34.

Compare this simple eagle with elaborate Baltimore examples.

32. *Below:* Appliqué album quilt, d. 1850, Maryland. "Mrs. Josiah Goodman, 1850″, embroidered on the back, indicates its probable maker. 94″ x 92¾″. Printed and plain cottons, wool, embroidery in various yarns. Bold meander and sawtooth borders and the omnipresent eagle tie the quilt to the Maryland album tradition.

19th century. Some symbols, of course, are obvious—the American eagle, the dove of peace, the dove of promise returning to the Ark with an olive branch. Ships are included on a few quilts, generally from Baltimore. While these sometimes refer to the trade of the recipient, quite often they are inscribed with "Hope" or "Zion," common religious references. And musical instruments might be depicted, particularly the harp and the lyre. Some were sacred and some profane, since harps might be found by women in a purely decorative or even mythological context in prints of trophies used in books, as furniture inlay, and on printed textiles.

Religious symbols are sometimes the straightforward Christian Cross, or, more often the anchor of hope. Bibles were occasionally appliquéd on Baltimore quilts, and may have been used elsewhere. The major fraternal orders—the Masons, established in America before 1730, and the Odd Fellows, established in 1813—also chose many Christian symbols to represent their orders. Many of these are found in quilt squares. Masonic blocks might feature the compass, three candles of the Trinity and their rite, aprons, trowels, and the lamp of knowledge. Odd Fellows were symbolized with three-linked chains—again a Trinity—and a heart and hand. The two orders shared the all-seeing eye, the beehive, and a number of other elements. Whether women chose to make blocks with these symbols to honor their husbands, fathers, or the recipient, or whether they were memorializing their own membership in the newly-formed womens' orders sometimes can be determined by the dates on dated quilts. The Order of the Eastern Star, a female Masonic order, and the Degree of Rebecca, part of the Odd Fellows fraternal order, were founded in 1850 and 1851, respectively.

33. *Left:* Appliqué album quilt top, unfinished, c. 1860-1870, Maryland, Baltimore area. Maker unknown. 84" x 84½ ". Printed and plain cottons.

34. *Above:* Appliqué album wedding quilt, c. 1857-1859, Manchester, Carroll County, Maryland. Made by Cornelia Everhart Wissler. 81" x 79". Cottons: ink details.

Many of the finest album quilts are enclosed in borders which hold the diverse squares together. Early Baltimore quilts, and quilts from other areas throughout the album period, might be surrounded by simple bands of turkey red — a plain but vibrant red cotton. Sashes were used to separate the squares in some quilts, giving relief from the overwhelming complexity in the album. Some quiltmakers were willing to forego the sashes, but left more white space in every square to achieve this effect. The more adventurous sometimes chose printed textiles to form the borders and sashes which separated the blocks. Another favorite was the elaborate floral meander border, made up of hundreds of pieces which were cut to represent flowers and leaves, then laid down in gentle curves and sewed in place. Successful planners managed to get the curves to work out carefully in the corners, but the novice quiltmaker might end with odd-shaped curves and loops at this critical point.

Swags, festoons, and bowknots are often found on printed chintzes and other printed textiles produced after the mid-1830s. These were adapted for the album border. Maryland quilts, and some made at the borders of the state, may feature these crescent-shaped swags alternating with a bow or a tassle, but the bows are not always included.

35. Appliqué album presentation quilt top, unfinished, d. 1852. Maker unknown. 97″ x 79½″. Printed and plain cottons, woven silk, velvet; ink and embroidery details and ink inscriptions. Inscribed in the lower left square: "Little Lucy/ from Fanny Walker/ Baltimore/ 1852". Other squares are signed in ink by members of the Dames, Gelbach, Barrenger, Brunner, Walker, Lambert, Scofeild, Bombarger, McCullough, and Brockhold families. A bunch of carrots appears in one of the four unusual corner squares. Compare these with the carrots in fig. 34. The corners here may each refer to some profession or aspiration of the recipient, recorded by Dunton as Captain Aust. The name "Little Lucy" refers to the heroine of a series of mid-19th-century children's books.

The Delaware-Chesapeake Album Tradition

Baltimore quilts were extraordinary, the distinctive product of a very small area. Yet quiltmakers throughout the region connected by rivers draining into the Delaware and Chesapeake Bays fashioned quilts that can be easily recognized today. The appliqué is bold and graphic, large motifs fill large squares, and cutwork techniques are frequently seen. Red and green small-figured prints dominate the quilters' palette. Throughout the region small local patterns developed within the larger design tradition.

36. Piecework and appliqué autograph quilt, d. 1842-1843, Pennsylvania, Philadelphia area. Probably made by Charlotte Gillingham and Phebe Ware Gilling-ham for Samuel Padgett Hancock, fiancé of Charlotte. 97¼ " x 127¼ ". Printed chintz, figured and plain cottons, silk, satin, and brocade; embroidery in silk and wool; ink inscriptions. Central wreath inscribed: "Fifth 1843 month/ Samuel P. Hancock". Inscriptions, with and without individual or paired signatures, appear in fifty-six

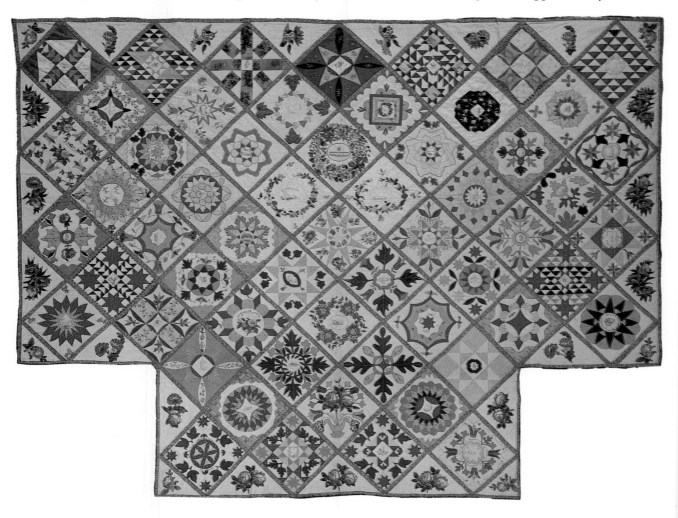

squares. Appliqué chintz and small Bowtie, Wild Goose Chase, and other triangle-form piecework patterns are mixed with appliqué squares of more conventional design. Several squares feature embroidery in Berlin-work patterns, popular from about 1830 to 1880. The similarity of techniques and repeat use of fabrics argue for one or two makers.

37. *Right top:* Appliqué album quilt, c. 1855, probably Pennsylvania, Lancaster County. Maker unknown. Printed and plain cottons; wool embroidery. The shield-bodied American eagle and bold leaf-form appliqué patterns are likely to be found on Pennsylvania quilts. A heart-shaped wreath, bouquets, and other floral tributes indicate the commemoration of a betrothal or wedding. The charming heart-and-hand square probably alludes to Odd Fellows membership of the prospective husband.

38. *Right:* Appliqué and piecework friendship album quilt, d. 1844 and 1852, New Brunswick area, New Jersey. Made by Francina Stout Van Dyke (1802-1885), Monmouth Junction, New Jersey. 101" x 88". Printed and plain cottons. Ink inscriptions include: "Mary Wlliamson/ Bound Brook", "Kate Van Dyke", "Mary A. Whitenack/ Blawenburgh, New Jersey/ April 1852", "Sophia A. Engler/ Raratuss", "Maria Thomas/ 1844", "Tresenlea", "Rebecca Van Dyke/ New Brunswick", "Maria Lausors/ Cedar Grove", "Maria Bennet/ Bound Brook", "Maria V. Brearley" and other Smiths and Van Dykes. This quilt descended in the family, remaining in the area where it was made until recently. A record of family and friends seems its purpose. Several of the appliqué squares feature the same boldly-cut leaf motifs popular in neighboring Pennsylvania.

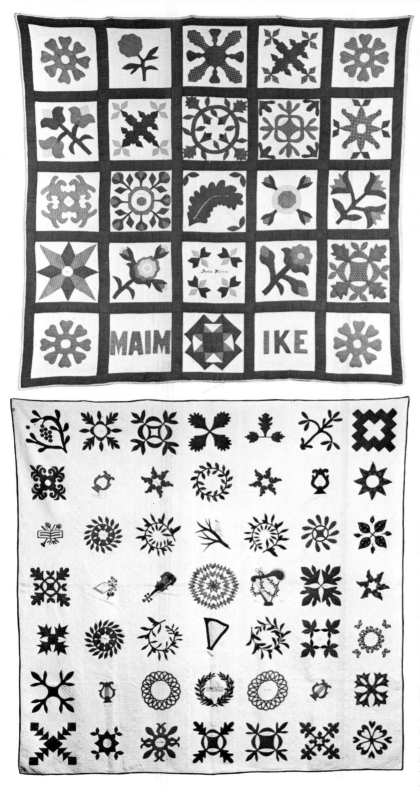

39. *Above left:* Appliqué album quilt, c. 1850, probably Pennsylvania. Made for or by Amelia Melchior, whose name is embroidered in red thread in one square. 78" x 78". Plain and printed cottons. Among the few other names inscribed in black ink on the squares are: "Sarah A. MvKeag" and "Sabile A. McKeag". The former may have been applied with rubber printing blocks and a slightly sidewise "v" used to represent a "c" needed for McKeag. Large appliqué block letters spell "MAIM" AND "IKE," leaving no doubt about the first names of those to be honored with this quilt, but its purpose is still conjectural. The two linked names have a famous parallel among 20th-century Pennsylvanians.

40. *Above right:* Detail of appliqué album coverlet, d. 1847, Ridley, Pennsylvania. Center inscription of quilt reads: "Ann L. Worrall/ Ridley Delaware Co PA 1847". 98" x 118". Printed and plain cottons. One of a pair of Pennsylvania shield-bodied eagles fly above an oversize cut-paper design central block. Repeated use of fabrics and similarity of design in this quilt suggest that one person, probably Ann Worrall, made it. Many squares are signed by men and women whose family names are still likely to be found in the area.

41. *Opposite bottom:* Appliqué and piecework musical album quilt, d. 1846, Pennsylvania, Oxford area. Maker unknown. Printed and plain cottons; silk embroidery, ink inscriptions. 97" x 92½". Harps and lyres, a violin, a crossed flute and clarinet, sheet music, and a songbird all express a musical theme, but this quilt raises more questions than it answers. Whether it was for a music teacher or made by a group that played together, and what sort of occasion is being celebrated, are questions shrouded in history.

42. *Right top:* Appliqué album quilt, d. 1860, Pennsylvania, probably Lancaster County. Inscribed in ink: "Hannah Wortendyke/ May 17th 1860". 82" x 81". Printed and plain cottons; wool, silk and cotton embroidery. Inscriptions in cross-stitch: "The Swallows/ M.E.", "Mrs. H. Perry", and "S.C." Many differences in stitches and textiles suggest that the quilt was not made by Hannah Wortendyke alone. It seems, instead, to be a true album collection of good wishes marking a betrothal. Flowers, hearts, cornucopias, and birds suggest felicitations, but is the wreath with the cat among the birds a warning?

43. *Right:* Appliqué album quilt top, unfinished, c. 1865, probably Pennsylvania. Maker unknown. 87" x 86". Printed and plain cottons; cotton embroidery, ink inscriptions. Nineteen names of the twenty-five women who signed this quilt are still legible, and their friendship and Christian fellowship are well recorded with flowers in baskets and vases, wreaths, hearts, the Cross, and the anchor of hope. One ingenious seamstress has created an oak tree from what must have been tracings of actual leaves.

44. *Left top:* Appliqué album quilt, c. 1860-1870, Baltimore, Maryland. Maker unknown. Plain and printed cottons; silk, cotton, and wool embroidery. One or possibly two needlewomen fashioned this bold design sampler album using some very lightweight cotton textiles. Extra stuffing behind flowers, fruit, and vases brings an added dimension to the charmingly naïve squares. The hand offering a bouquet is unique.

45. *Left:* Appliqué album quilt, d. 1859, Maryland, just below the Pennsylvania border. Maker unknown. 85" x 95". Printed and plain cottons; wool and cotton embroidery. All names are embroidered on the quilt. In center block: ink drawing of a bird carrying a love letter beneath inked initials "N.E.B."; at bottom of square is embroidered: "February 5th 1859/ Nick." Also on quilt are the names "Janney Barker", "Sarah Barker", "February 14, 1859/ Hannah M. Boyd", "Jenney Barker", "Wm N. P. Boyd/ March 6, 1859" and "C. D. J. Boyd". All of which points to a hopeful family welcoming a new wife. Rare foliate sashes and a swag with bowknot border enclose this charming gift of love.

46. *Opposite page:* Appliqué album quilt, d. 1852, Pennsylvania, Chambersburg area. Probably made for or by Martha H[?]oach, who inscribed one square "Martha H[?]oach/ Chambersburg, Pennsylvania/ March 18th 1852". 79" x

81½". Plain and printed cottons and linen; wool and silk embroidery. "Mrs. Clara Crevensten" added her name in cross-stitch to the glorious broken wreath. "Mary M. Crevensten" also signed in cross-stitch. "Mary Echols/ Shepherdstown", "Emily Ann Hart", and Rebecca [illegible]/ March 18th/ 1852" added inked inscriptions. Much of the dark blue-green seems to have come from the same stock of fine home-dyed plain-weave linen. Ruched flowers add texture to the broken wreath, while a sprinkling of hearts suggests a marriage about to be celebrated.

Other Large-Square Quilts

Outside the Delaware-Chesapeake region, album quilts took on a different look. Red and green still predominated, possibly because fabrics in these colors were readily available and the combination was striking. The few New England albums have all the linear quality and attenuation of furniture from that area. Women in other places fashioned quilts which seem sparse or perhaps too busy if compared with the Chesapeake album. Each coverlet must be examined on its own for clues to the background of its maker.

47. *Opposite page:* Appliqué album quilt, c. 1860, American. Maker unknown. 80″ x 82″. Plain and printed cottons. Ink inscriptions. This fascinating and puzzling quilt may have been made in New Jersey, judging from the combination of small-square format and Chesapeake appliqués in some blocks. Domestic symbols like the cat, coffeepot, and hearts mix with patriotic flags and shields. Fraternal and religious motifs dominate. Most have Odd Fellows connotations. Nearly every square contains a Cross in one form or another.

48. *Right top:* Appliqué marriage quilt, mid-19th century, New England. Maker unknown. 93″ x 96″. Printed and plain cottons; silk embroidery. Ink inscriptions include in two places the initials of the recipients, "A.R. and G.R." The linear quality and open ground show New England design traditions. Hens replace a more usually seen dove, and a bowl of fruit looks suspiciously like a bowl of eggs. Where hearts are not used in appliqué, wedding rings or hearts are worked in quilting.

49. *Right:* Appliqué album quilt, c. 1850, Newport, Indiana, or Clinton County, Ohio. Maker unknown. 70″ x 72″. Printed and plain cottons; ink inscriptions. Most likely one maker fashioned this delicate and open quilt, and friends signed it. Each square shows design affinity with its neighbor. The appliqué cherries are all stuffed. All fourteen signatures are accompanied by some notation of the signer's hometown, now confused by the name change of Newport to Fountain City after the quilt was made.

50. Appliqué album quilt, d. 1855, Virginia. Maker unknown. 86" x 85". Printed and plain cottons. An unusual color scheme combines with some bold appliqué and cut-work designs of the Chesapeake tradition. Corner squares of the border yellow are pieced with white sashes to divide the blocks.

51. Appliqué album quilt, mid-19th century, Ohio or eastern Indiana. Maker unknown. 106" x 114". Printed and plain cottons. Brilliant floral tributes and a lively Odd Fellows square mark this midwestern quilt. Repeat use of the same solid red, and the green—found in the sashes and many leaves—indicate a single anonymous maker. This quilt was undoubtedly made after 1851, when the Degree of Rebecca was established. Symbols of the women's degree—the dove, moon, and stars—are included with those of a fully initiated male of the Scarlet Degree. Since many symbols overlap, it is difficult to say whom this quilt honored.

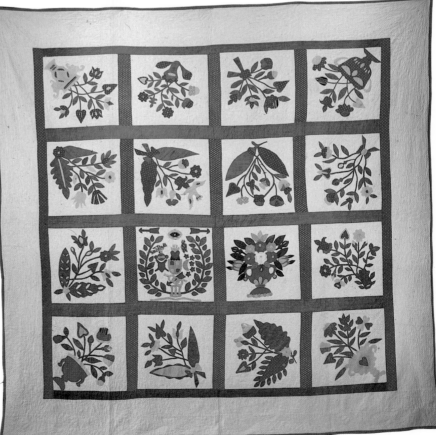

52. Appliqué marriage quilt, c. 1840-1850, Virginia, Staunton area. Maker unknown. 94" x 92½". Printed and plain cottons. A delightful "wild" quilt with irregular meander borders of natural and very stylized leaves and conventionalized flowers. The center square offers a very personal view of the bridal couple—the groom complete with military epaulets—inside a wreath. Chesapeake cutwork and appliqué with ties to the Pennsylvania-German design tradition show the influence of these settlers of the Valley of Virginia. Masonic emblems fill the lower-right square.

An End to the Album Tradition

The album fad ended by about 1870, and late quilts show the influence of new needlework fashions. Some can scarcely be distinguished from the crazy quilt, the next distinct type of coverlet to evolve. A few women simply continued to make quilts in conventional patterns. After all, the reasons for making an album still remained. Others revived them at a much later time. Most of the small-square quilts were made during the last quarter of the 19th century.

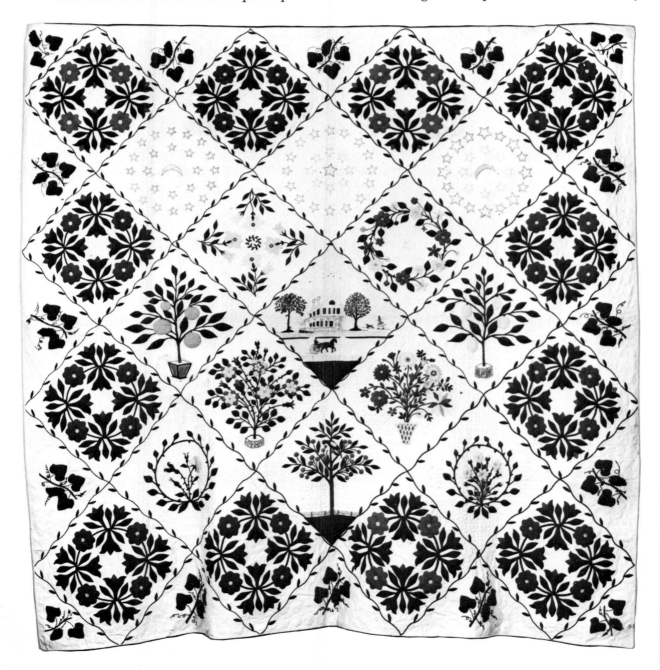

53. *Opposite page:* Appliqué album quilt, c. 1860-1865, East Orange, New Jersey. Made by Emeline Dean-Jones. 92″ x 92″. Printed and plain cottons; silk embroidery. Centered in the quilt is the Dean-Jones home, built in 1856 with wide Victorian porches. Potted shrubs and a tree are arranged around the bottom of the house, and the stars and moon shine above it. Stuffed-work emphasizes many flowers and fruits, buttonhole stitch outlines most of the appliqué. Intricate quilting—a different pattern in nearly every square—completes an extraordinary quilt.

54. *Right top:* Appliqué album quilt, c. 1880, Hackensack, New Jersey. Probably made for and finished by S.H. Randall, who may have been engaged to a Demarest family member. 82″ x 90″. Printed and plain cottons; silk embroidery, embroidered and inked inscriptions. A small-square quilt with elaborate lattice sets, this friendship medley has a little of everything: scissors cutting out a shirt, a pleasant home (made of the same fabric as the set), the anchor, a knotted ribbon, hearts, a horseshoe for luck, a locomotive, and two different scenes from "H.M.S. Pinafore." Demarest and Randall names are featured in the inscriptions.

55. *Right:* Appliqué album coverlet, last quarter 19th century, found in New Hampshire. Maker unknown, 1890. Plain cottons; silk embroidery. Use of the same fabric and similar heart or clover and arrow appliqué motif strongly indicate a single maker. A wonderful menagerie of birds and animals races through the squares. Several crazy quilt techniques, particularly the feather stitch on the sashes, help date the spread.

56. Appliqué album quilt, d. 1881, New York. Makers unknown. 81″ x 70″. Just outside the small-square dimensions, this quilt still has the compressed feel of that type coverlet. The parishioners and friends of the Rev. J. F. Jones made this presentation quilt, complete with rebus in the lower-right corner. Inclusion of a rebus—the combination of words and pictures to spell a message—is very rare. This says "No cross/ No crown."

57. Appliqué and piecework album coverlet, mid-19th century, New York State. Maker unknown. 76″ x 86″. Plain and printed cottons; silk embroidery. Piecework initials in the corners, "L A" and "B [?] B," probably signify a wedding. The brilliant green of the borders, sashes, and some appliqué comes from one dye lot, probably home-mixed. It is likely that this splen-did coverlet was a gift from the bride to the groom. The birds and bouquets are particularly charming.

58. Appliqué album quilt, early 1900s, Staten Island, New York. Made by the Beacon Light Chapter, Order of the Eastern Star. 87" x 72½". Red and green plain cotton; silk embroidery. Masonic emblems appear in each of the thirty squares. Needlework in this revival piece is uniformly excellent, though several members con-tributed to this gift for the Chapter's sponsors, Beacon Light Lodge. The squares were quilted separately and later joined together.

59. *Above:* Appliqué and piecework album coverlet, late 19th-early 20th century, Landis Valley, Pennsylvania. Plain and printed cottons; cotton embroidery. Extraordinary trapunto, or stuffed, fruit and flowers, meander sashes and border grace an unusual late coverlet.

60. *Right top:* Appliqué and piecework album quilt, c. 1910, Michigan, Gaines Township (near Flint). Made by Birdie Perry and friends. 66″ x 93″. Printed and plain cottons; various embroidery materials. Remembrances and good luck wishes mix with hearts and some piecework patterns. This continues the album tradition and is not a revival. Here, turn-of-the-century embroidered squares combine with album blocks which might easily have been done by any needlewoman fifty years earlier.

61. *Right:* Appliqué and piecework album crib quilt, c. 1950, American. Made by Florence Peto. 45½″ x 36½″. Printed and plain cottons. Florence Peto, one of the most important researchers of quilts, made this revival crib quilt—a sampler incorporating many traditional patterns. The meander border is skillfully worked.

62. Piecework and appliqué friendship quilt, d. 1849, 1850, New York, probably Hempstead, Long Island. Made by Margaret Cleland and friends. 100″ x 101″. Printed and plain cottons; ink inscriptions. The diagonal sashes and border half-squares are made from an English printed cotton which mimicked the pieced quilt pattern, Baby's Blocks. (First introduced about the time this quilt was put together, these fabrics provided a shortcut substitute for elaborate piecing.) An appliqué chintz square and an appliqué chinoiserie figure of an opium-smoking man at the center complement pieced and appliqué patterns. Eliza Woods, Jane L. Betts, Mary Banks, Bridget Kur-man, Cousin Julia and others signed squares. One friend added a Gaelic verse in one corner which translates: "Sad it is, O fair little sampler,/ Over thy flat surface one will say:/'The hand that wrote it does not survive.'" Even the name Mary Epworthy was rendered in Gaelic.

3. "A Token of Friendship": The American Friendship Quilt

Friendship quilts, too, were made with a variety of techniques. Early ones were block quilts. That was not always the case by the end of the 19th century. Like album quilts, friendship quilts were appliquéd, or pieced, or combinations of techniques. The array of signatures and their intentions make them different from the album. While the album quilt was competitive, the friendship quilt was less so. More often than not, a friendship quilt had a single pattern and a single maker. Friends were invited to inscribe their names and a verse or small drawing after the quilt top was finished. They may have then quilted the piece as a group. The project was truly a friendship offering and a record of time and memories shared—more homely, in both senses of the word, than the brilliant album. If it was simpler, it was just as comforting.

But several of these tops were quilted long after they were made. It is easy to imagine the last-minute preparations for moving or a wedding interfering with the quilting job at hand. Some were never put together at all. The quilt top is all that remains—carefully preserved for sentiments, not warmth.

Certain small geographic areas were likely to develop one particular pattern. In fact, discrete regional styles often appear within a county or group of towns. Here, a pattern might flourish for a generation and then die out as the novelty of another pattern took hold. Occasionally, specific designs migrated when one woman moved to a new community, introduced her pattern, and was rewarded by its adoption in the new location. Quilts migrated, too, so isolated examples of one regional style might show up in an unexpected place. Americans kept moving, carrying their quilts and quilt patterns with them.

Other patterns became so disseminated that they later gained a second name. The Chimney Sweep, for example, is often called "the Friendship Block." Quilts in this pattern were made from Vermont to Oregon, and hundreds of variants appeared. The piecing is simple, and large white centers in these blocks lend themselves very readily to the inscriptions the genre demands. Even this pattern, however, received distinct treatment in certain areas. A number of towns in central New York produced Chimney Sweep quilts with dark-ground printed textiles. These look so similar that one can immediately place them in that region.

Pennsylvanians in the Lehigh Valley and elsewhere in the eastern half of the state often chose the Reel pattern for friendship quilts. A few examples of a stylized fleur-de-lis appliqué motif have also appeared in family record and friendship quilts. In Chester County, the design of choice was a variant on a fundamental block, often set on the diagonal. This pattern and a nine-patch version of it have shown up in New Jersey quilts from the Princeton-Hopewell area and in at least one spread from Lebanon County, Pennsylvania.

Friendship quilts seem to have remained popular for a long time. While most of the classic albums were only made for about two decades, 1840-1860, friendship quilts, in one guise or another, were made well into the 20th century. The most desirable, however, are the early pieces. These are filled with the sentiments and wishes of makers whom we can hardly trace, but their careful needlework, choice of textiles, and patterns are meaningful in their own right.

Often the quilts can speak. A number of these coverlets are family records, poignantly telling of births and deaths in a family. The center square of fig. 68 asks: "How many of us ere another year?/ May sleep beneath the cold and silent sod?/ Then while our lives, are in merce lengthened here,/ Let us in time, prepare to meet our God." Surrounding the center star are birth and death dates of family members. Sadly, many are infants, one "10 months and 12 days" old. Similar records are found in many friendship quilts.

Leave-taking was not the only occasion for a friendship quilt. Weddings provided the same exciting opportunity they had for the classical album. Inscriptions in marriage quilts conveyed good wishes, both in words and in the small drawings which frequently livened a square. Bouquets and garlands, diminutive cabins, turtledoves in nests, pairs of doves at fountains, and, oddly enough, beehives and squirrels with nuts were likely candidates. These last two, found also on the album quilt, had particular significance for a viewer in the 19th century. The beehive signified industry. Whole books were written about the life of bees, which young people received as gifts for moral instruction. The meaning of the squirrel, however, has been lost.

Family reunions and funerals, though the latter seems a somewhat grim but frequent occasion, provided other opportunities for women to get together and create a quilt. The transportation of the era made gathering friends and family difficult, so advantage was taken when these opportunities presented themselves. One can imagine an enterprising family member bringing along her scraps and cautioning others to do the same if a reunion was in the offing. Several of the quilts in this section seem to have sprung from just such inspiration.

To render the reunion indelible for the future, names and drawings on quilts were inscribed with the permanent inks that came on the market after about 1845. Before these inks were available, homemade recipes had to serve. Some inks, of course, have proved more durable than others.

63. *Above left:* Appliqué friendship quilt, d. 1846, 1848. Pennsylvania, Chester County. Made by Mary Preston, perhaps as a wedding gift. 103" x 93". Printed and plain cottons; ink inscriptions. Stylized fleurs-de-lis enclose signatures of men and women in Plum Grove, Philadelphia and Wilmington, Delaware. All signers were Friends, or Quakers.

64. *Above right:* Detail, appliqué friendship quilt, d. 1846, Pennsylvania. Maker unknown. 96" x 96½". Printed and plain cottons; ink inscriptions. Oak leaves, a symbol of long life and honor in the 19th century, surround verses and signatures from well-wishers and friends. This quilt was brought to Wisconsin with a family that moved there.

65. *Left:* Appliqué and piecework family record quilt, c. 1866, Pennsylvania, Doylestown area. Made by a member of the Darlington family. 89½" x 89". Printed and plain cottons; ink inscriptions. Pennsylvanians seemed fond of the fleur-de-lis and usually cut the motif from one piece of fabric. Here, all sorts of turkey-red calicos frame the names and birth (and occasionally death) dates of members of the Darlington family. The names were inscribed by two or, possibly, more hands.

66. *Above:* Piecework and appliqué quilt, c. 1845, Pennsylvania, Chester County. Maker unknown. 90" x 103". Printed and plain cottons; ink inscriptions. A large group of Chester County quilts feature this variation of the fundamental block pattern, though few have added appliqué borders or color harmonies like this particular example. Perhaps this served as a fund-raising quilt, since there are a large number of repeat signatures. Thomas Bald-win's name appears three times; Norris Wilkinson, Ruel N. Jefferies, John Welchwood, John McElhaney and Jonathan J. Woodward are each named on two squares.

67. *Right:* Detail of the center square of fig. 68.

68. Appliqué and piecework family record coverlet, c. 1845-1850, Pennsylvania, possibly Lebanon County. Maker unknown. 99" x 99". Printed and plain cottons; ink inscriptions. Brilliant printed cottons from the middle of the 19th century are pieced in the fundamental block pattern common to Chester County. Several squares feature ripple prints found in Baltimore album quilts, but most are the small figured prints of the period. The Snyder family name and central tulip appliqué suggest a Pennsylvania-German influence. Signatures in squares include: "Amanda Snyder—July 1845; Elizabeth Duffield; Jones Duffield; Mary Griffith; P. Enyard; J.A. Enyard; Phebe Snyder; Maria T. Wilson Todd; Joseph Vandergris[?]t; Theodore Vandergris[?]t; and M.A. Thackard."

69. *Right:* Piecework and appliqué friendship quilt, c. 1850, New Jersey, Hopewell area. Maker unknown. 78″ x 78″. Printed and plain cottons; ink inscriptions. A diagonal set turns this fundamental block into the Chimney Sweep pattern. In the half-squares created by the diagonal set, the quilt-maker has placed stylized flower sprays and leaves, some cut from plain turkey-red cotton.

70. *Below:* Piecework friendship quilt, mid-19th century, Enosburgh Falls, Vermont. Made by Mrs. Esther Irish. 85″ x 84¾″. Plain and printed cottons; ink inscriptions. Green calico was used for this Duck's-Foot-in-the Mud pattern pieced quilt. Other names for the pattern are Bear's Paw or Hand of Friendship. Mrs. Irish made this quilt before she moved to Iowa and had her Vermont friends sign remembrance squares.

71. *Above:* Detail of piecework wedding quilt, d. 1843, Pennsylvania, Chester County. Maker unknown. 98″ x 94″. Printed and plain cottons; ink inscriptions and stencil. Red calicos and white muslin are pieced in a Weather Vane pattern. This quilt was never used. Two different chalked quilting patterns are still clearly drawn on the face. Signatures are usually accompanied by a drawing.

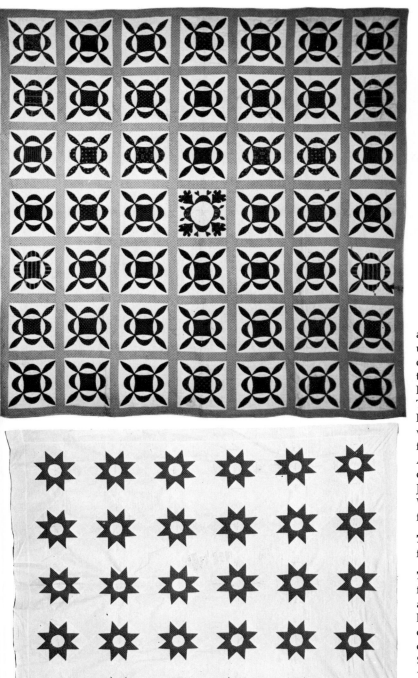

and red Reel appliqué blocks are used in this vibrant spread. The occasion for the quilt is unclear, as the inscribed center Oak-Leaf-and-Reel reads: "When the last loud Trump shall sound/ To wake the King of terrors/ Then may this work in Heaven be found/ A cloak for all my errors" — a potent verse. A single hand has entered names of men and women of the Jack, Jackson, Rolliston, Livezey, Woodard, Roberts and Gill families.

73. *Above:* Detail of center square of fig. 72.

74. *Left:* Piecework quilt top, unfinished, d. 1859, American, probably Pennsylvania. Maker unknown. 86" x 74". Plain and printed cottons; ink inscriptions. Green calico is pieced in the LeMoyne Star pattern with a center listing "To The Dead," and one "To The Living" of the Hemler family, all of whom were "Borned" between 1833 and 1843. This quilt was presented to Mrs. Hemler, departing from Meadville. The inscriptions are in several hands. The LeMoyne Star pattern was not a common one for friendship quilts.

72. *Above top:* Appliqué friendship quilt, d. September 30, 1850, Pennsylvania, probably Chester County. Made by Enzia Jackson. 83" x 83". Printed and plain cottons; ink inscriptions. Brilliant yellow sashes

75. Piecework friendship quilt, c. 1850, American, possibly Pennsylvania. Maker unknown. 81" x 80". Printed and plain cottons; ink stamps and stencils. This Chimney Sweep or Memory Block quilt makes good use of a restricted palette of red, deep-green and chrome-yellow calico. Each center cross holds a name—some stamped and others cut as part of the stenciled oval cartouche enclosing the name. Use of these shortcuts led to upside-down letters and hasty spelling, or perhaps misspelling, of names. The quilt includes signatures of: "SUSANNA. C. BOORSE. JOHN. K. BOARSE., SARAH.. KRATZ., ANNA SEIPT., ELIZABETH. B. BEYER., DANIEL.K. BOARSE., CALHARINE..METZ., and MARY. LANDES."

76. Stencil plate, last half of the 19th century, American. Made for Annie R. Hahn. The stencil itself was a craft form in the 19th century. Plates were typically cut by tinsmiths for use in labels and decoration of all sorts. Stencilwork is often found on friendship quilts. The novelty of the fad was appealing, and stenciling was far easier than drawing small mementos or repeating popular designs. Moreover, the same brass stencils used to create these motifs on quilts worked just as well on stationery and album books. Some caligraphic signatures were also reproduced in stencil. A thick black ink, rather like printers' ink, was pushed through the cutout area with a stubby brush. After it dried, no amount of laundering would ever completely remove it. In the second half of the century, rubber stamps of single letters became fashionable. These blocky letters are easily recognized.

77. Piecework presentation quilt, d. November 22d, 1854, Kennett Square, Pennsylvania. Made by Sallie Annie Forwood for her mother, Hannah Warner (1811-1866). 91" x 91". Printed and plain cottons; ink inscriptions. Signed in the center, "Sallie Annie Forwood./ Kennett Square/ November 22d/ 1854". This unusual LeMoyne Star quilt was a family gift. Relatives and friends inked their names: "Issachar Edwin Hoopes, Edward & Lizzie Warner, Smithson Forwood, Alexander & Hannah E. Ran[way], and Thomas & Jane Brinton" were among the signers.

78. Appliqué and piecework remembrance quilt, d. 1873, possibly Pennsylvania. Made by Fiona Wertman. 100½" x 91". Printed and plain cottons; inked inscriptions. Deep maroon, turkey red, blue, and mustard yellow surround the inscriptions of several members of different families added to this quilt, among them men and women named Freyman, Gilbert, Peter, Ebbert, Koons, Lauchenor, and several Wertmans. The name of Fiona Wertman, centered at the bottom, is over a flourished cartouche surrounding the date "1873". Perhaps this quilt was signed at a family reunion.

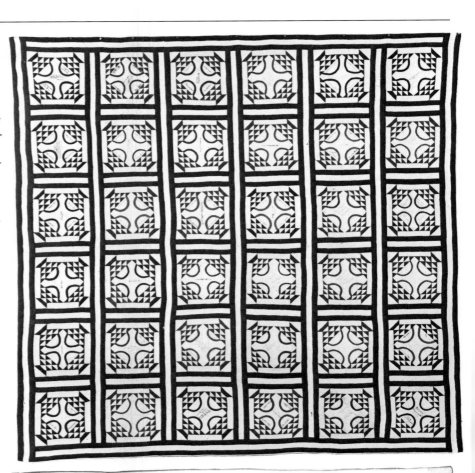

79. Piecework presentation quilt, c. 1860-1862, New Vernon, New Jersey. Made by the congregation of the First Presbyterian Church of New Vernon, New Jersey. Red and white cotton and cotton tapes; inked inscriptions. Pieced baskets surround the inked names, verses, and drawings done by the ladies of the congregation for their minister, Reverend Elias N. Crane. Baskets and handles face each other in each square, leaving a cross outlined in the center. Quilts were frequent gifts for departing ministers. Signers of this one added a verse from Psalm 126: "He that goeth forth and/ weepeth, bearing precious/ seed shall doubtless/ come again with rejoicing,/ bringing his sheaves with him."

80. *Right:* Piecework remembrance or presentation quilt, d. 1852, Pennsylvania, Butler County. Maker unknown. 85" x 85". Indigo blue and white plain cottons; inked inscription. Feathered Stars surrounded by a zigzag border are even more lively because crossed center pieces were added in a single Irish Chain. Along one edge is a small inked inscription: "C.P. Anderson/ Butler Co., Pa./ December 22, 1852/ Remember me."

81. *Below:* Piecework friendship or remembrance quilt, c. 1890, Pennsylvania, probably Lancaster County. Maker unknown. 94" x 78". Printed and plain cottons; ink applied with letter rubber stamps. Rose, blue, and yellow small-figure prints predominate in this Rolling Stone pattern quilt. Names from the Hamaker, Sahm, Eichelberger, Shelley, Hummer, Singer, Scruh, Miller, Glassly, and Youtz families are represented, but Sahms are most numerous. Letters, here, are individually stamped—probably after the blocks were assembled. Intricate quilting embellishes borders and sashes.

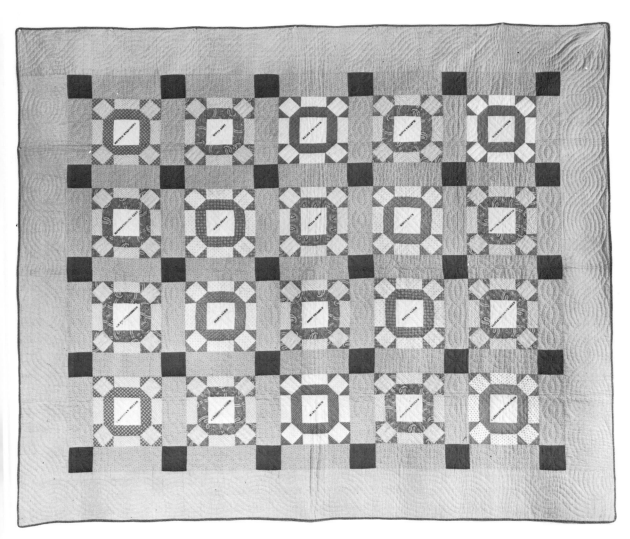

82. *Above:* Piecework family record quilt square, c. 1840, probably New Hampshire. Possibly made by Ebenezer and Betsy Rollins. 16⅞″ x 16¾″. Red and white plain cottons: ink inscriptions. Triangular and diamond-shaped pieces are joined around a circular center to complete a sunburst quilt block. Elaborate caligraphic leaves mark every family entry, while gesturing hands emphasize each corner. The ornate penmanship, popular at that time, was probably the husband's contribution to his wife's artful piecework.

83. *Left:* Detail of fig. 84, family record quilt square, d. 1842. Possibly inscribed by Caspar Wistar Pennock. Recent generations of the Pennock and Morris families were carefully detailed on facing pages of an open book. The legend "C.W. Pennock/ to his/ Daughter./ 1842." is on the book spine.

84. Piecework marriage quilt top, unfinished, d. 1842, 1843, Pennsylvania, Marlborough Township, Chester County. Made for Sarah Pennock. 66" x 66". Printed and plain cottons; ink drawings and inscriptions. Paper templates on the back, each numbered, identify piecing patterns for elaborate star and pinwheel designs. Notice how carefully printed textiles have been cut to emphasize pinwheel effects and balanced motifs in stars. Sarah Pennock apparently married a Lukens—perhaps a cousin—on "3 mo 21. 1842" (March 21). Other Pennocks, Wollastons, Gibbonses and Lukenses added signatures to drawings of doves, cornucopias, ships, shells, eagles, and, in one, crossed flags topped by a liberty cap. Although one person probably made the quilt top, the whole family contributed to this elegant gift which, sadly, was never quilted.

85. Piecework quilt, d. 1859, New York, Pierstown area. Maker unknown. 78¼" x 75½". Printed and plain cottons; ink inscriptions. Used by the Doubleday family, this quilt contains signatures from families in the Cooperstown area—McEwan, Ingalls, and several dated squares from Margaret Patten. It displays many of the regional characteristics of an upstate New York Chimney Sweep friendship quilt—rich, dark printed cottons, large center crosses, and a similarity of overall design. Sashes are of red and white polka-dot fabric.

86. Piecework friendship quilt, c. 1855, New York, Scipioville area. Maker unknown. 83" x 73". Printed and plain cottons; ink inscriptions. One or two people added the inscriptions to this classic upstate New York Chimney Sweep quilt. Blocks of cone or "paisley" print on blue-gray ground alternate with pattern squares in remarkably brilliant earthtones. Blocks were inscribed by Hannah Hoxie, of Scipioville, and a number of husbands and wives in surrounding New York communities. "Fred & Anna Coleman/ Passaic, NJ" and "Horace G. Howland/ Cleveland/ Ohio" were among the contributors from far away. Perhaps a family reunion was in progress when the quilt was fashioned.

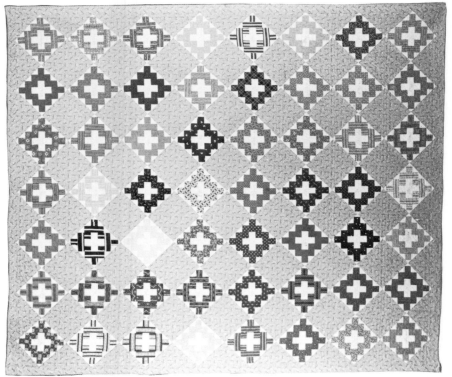

87. Detail of piecework family remembrance or autograph quilt top, d. 1874, American, possibly Wisconsin. Maker unknown. Printed and plain cottons; ink inscriptions. 68" x 84". A variant of the Chimney Sweep holds inked verses and signatures of the Sawyer and Jewell families and their friends.

88. Piecework quilt, d. 1850, 1851, Pennsylvania, Stonersville, Berks County. Probably made by Martha Lee. 96" x 96". Printed and plain cottons and satin; ink inscriptions and stencil. Subtle dark colors, pieced in the Ohio Star pattern, emphasize the plain beliefs held by the Quaker woman who fashioned this quilt. It was inscribed by members of the Lee, Wright, Chrisman, and Thomas families,

among others. Three blocks include town names—Chesterfield, Ohio, and Amity, Pennsylvania. One for Ellen Brimfield, who apparently died in 1851 at age 77, contains the Longfellow verse: "Art is long and time is/ fleeting. And our hearts/ tho stout and brave. Still/ like muffled drums are/ beating Funeral marches/ to the Grave."

89. Detail of fig. 88, showing use of a stencil—a surprising vanity for a Quaker.

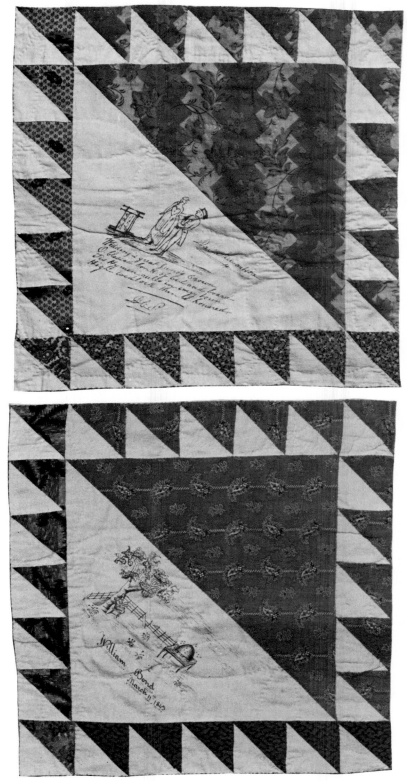

90. *Above left:* Detail of fig. 93. David Stewartson inscribed these epithalemic wishes for the bride-to-be, an anonymous Mary: "Wedding is great Juno's Crown/ O blessed bond of bed and board/ Tis Hymen rules in every town/ High wedlock then be honored." Among various pieces of advice to Mary is Cornelia E. Slack's entry dated "Octr: 1843" — "Give me but sense, a taste refined./ Candor with honor blended,/ A feeling heart, a virtuous mind,/ with charity attended." This reflects the sensibility of the mid-19th century, as does the inscription of John N. Slack, also dated in October of 1843: "Reason's whole pleasure, all the joys of sense,/ Lie in three words, health, peace and competence." And Sarah H. Slack added more moral advice: "To Mary/ Come with virtue at thy side/ And religion for a guide/ Ask and you will be forgiven/ Seek and find a home in heaven". This verse was dated March 6th 1839—the earliest of the quilt. So many members of the Slack family added signatures that one must suppose they were either Mary's family or her prospective family.

91. *Opposite page, above right:* Detail of fig. 93, a curious drawing of a man at a lathe or some similar machine, perhaps mirroring the occupation of the groom.

92. *Opposite page, below:* Detail of fig. 93. The beehive of industry

was always appropriate for a marriage quilt.

93. *Above:* Piecework marriage quilt, d. 1839, 1842, 1843, American, probably New England. Maker unknown. 94½" x 104". Printed and plain cottons; ink in-

scriptions. This vibrant quilt combines Two Patch and Sawtooth piecing. Most squares are inscribed "To Mary", and many contain some message, verse, or drawing like those shown in figs. 90-92.

94. Piecework friendship quilt, c. 1895, Central Point, Oregon. Maker unknown. 79″ x 59″. Printed, check-weave, and plain cottons; cotton embroidery. A late Chimney Sweep quilt in a subdued palette of light-green check and muted dress prints holds script-embroidered names of Mary, Minnie, and Suzy Moore, Mallie E. Cradock, Ellen N. and Alta M. Wood, Mary A. Turnidge, Elizabeth Miller, Katie Flemming, and Mary A. Kelsoe.

95. *Right:* Detail of piecework quilt, c. 1930, Madison, Wisconsin. Made by Mrs. Ward and other members of the 5th Ward Women's Sewing Society, Madison. During the Depression, interest in quilts revived as did simple patterns like variants of a fundamental block—the progenitor of the Chimney Sweep pattern. This quilt is pieced in soft pastels, so typical of the era.

96. Detail of fig. 98. In this quilt made for Lizzie Roberts, shirt and dress fabrics of the early 1880s are pieced in the Snowflake pattern. Each of the 72 block centers holds a message, best expressed by Amelda Eaton, who offered "A good wish for the quilt/ June 9, 1883". Almost every friend provided a name, hometown, and the date, while several added some special remembrance. Eva B. Justhises, Berta Judkins, Ida M. Havertress and Clara E. Harvill added "Your friend". All but Clara were from Athens, Maine, and wrote between June and December of 1883. "Think of Me" was added by E. Jennie Berry. Mrs. Mary Pooler of Palmyra, Maine, added "August 9, 1883/ Age 81½ years".

97. Piecework fund-raising quilt, d. 1887, Crossroads, Indiana. Made by the Womens' Home & Foreign Mission Society, Richwood Lutheran Church, Crossroads, Indiana. 86" x 74". Printed and plain cottons; cotton embroidery and ink inscriptions. Blue figured prints are used for the Chimney Sweep blocks which alternate with plain squares quilted in a feathered wreath design. Pieced blocks are signed with yellow embroidery, and approximately 150 additional names are added in ink. Five of those include the title "Reverend," suggesting that the "W.H. & F.M. Society" — as the group signed itself in one white block—tapped everyone who could possibly contribute to this project.

98. Piecework remembrance quilt, d. 1883, 1884, 1889, Maine, Gorham area. Made for Lizzie Roberts. 80" x 90". Printed and plain cottons. The story of this quilt may never be known. Blocks were made for Lizzie Roberts, who was apparently planning to move to Minnesota —and signed one block "LIZZIE/ MINN/ 1884". A year earlier Lizzie had signed a square in Gorham, Maine. Several Robertses including "Your sister/ Annie C. Roberts/ South Solon, Maine" had signed. "A. Roberts" added a Delton, Minnesota, hometown in 1884. The quilt blocks were not sewn together until 1914, when Hazel R. Porter joined them, added her name and "Alton, Maine/ year 1914." Rather than quilt the top, Hazel Porter tied threads through the layers—a tufting technique far easier than quilting. Did Lizzie really go to Minnesota?

99. Piecework friendship quilt, d. "12/27, 1927", "3/19/35", found in Louisville, Kentucky. Maker unknown. 82" x 71". Printed and plain cottons; cotton embroidery. Each block of this Chimney Sweep pattern quilt holds a single name embroidered in various colored cotton threads with dates from 1927 and 1935. Pastel fabrics mark its Depression-era origin. The quilting appears to have been done fairly recently, since the back and batting appear to be polyester. The quilting is somewhat crude and free-form, not stitched in an organized design.

100. Piecework presentation quilt, c. 1870, Pennsylvania. Maker unknown. 82" x 92". Printed and plain cottons. The striking Hourglass pattern blocks are optically dazzling when combined with Two-Patch squares. Hundreds of contributors have added their names in the white areas.

4. "Tasteful Works of Ceaseless Variety": The Late 19th-Century Ideal

The fad for album quilts ended before America's Centennial. Styles had changed drastically, and lives, too, changed with the demands of a pervasive industrial revolution. This was especially true in urban areas where well-read women, spurred by *Godey's Ladies' Book* and Catharine Beecher, made domestic accomplishments paramount. New needlework trends were introduced, flourished, then died out, while quilts and other coverlets continued to be made. Nights were still cold; bed covers were always needed. More important, these spreads continued to provide a useful medium for fancy and plain needlework—a display of a competence which women had to have. Quilts were evidence of a woman's commitment to the home, her desire to embellish it. Moreover, the social function of the quilt was never lost. Here was the perfect opportunity to meet with friends without feeling guilty for frivolity or wasting time. In fact, quiltmaking was a genteel accomplishment, rewarding in every possible way.

Toward the end of the album quilt's popularity, women began making sampler quilts. Some of these were a show of proficiency; some were records of favorite patterns, left to instruct posterity. Most sampler quilts of the day were piecework, but some combined appliqué techniques with pieced squares. Silks and velvets were favored materials in urban areas. The rural woman continued to work in cottons.

The crazy quilt phenomenon was the second form of the album quilt fad to flourish in the 19th century. Although they are far removed from the classical album, crazy quilts should be added to that class. Most crazy quilts were worked in blocks; each square was different; and these pieces often served as presentations for friends and relatives. The intentions of the makers were perhaps somewhat self-serving. These were decorative spreads in the truest sense, for women, themselves, were to *look* decorative while creating this "ornamental patchwork." When busily stitching, a woman was a focus of ideal domesticity, and magazines recommended she embellish a piece to the utmost. As the April, 1883 issue of *Godey's* suggested, "The greater the diversity in stitches the better..."

101. *Opposite page:* Piecework and appliqué sampler quilt, c. 1860, probably Connecticut. Maker unknown. 82" x 60". Plain and printed cottons. Indigo and light-blue small-figured prints combine in a balanced design sampler. Sixteen-Patch squares anchor the corners, while the center is filled with diamond and triangle-based blocks. Appliqué motifs break up any geometric rigidity.

Because the virtues of crazy quilts were widely disseminated by the popular magazines, and because they appealed to the "scrap bag mentality" American women cherished, this genre gathered converts with a vengeance. Many of these puzzle patchwork pieces, as they were sometimes called, featured some motif or theme to tie them together. A particularly charming Vermont quilt (fig. 115) is truly an album of animals and vignettes of family life. Other popular themes were botanical collections of embroidered plants or painted flowers, and children's occupations rendered in outline stitch and reminiscent of Kate Greenaway's endearing illustrations. Though seemingly unplanned, these coverlets required considerable organization.

The single most important influence on the crazy quilt appeared at the Centennial Exhibition in Philadelphia. This 1876 version of a World's Fair introduced thousands of Americans to Japanese arts and crafts. The Japanese style was instantly adopted in the already ecclectic Victorian design vocabulary and showed up as fans, in small motifs, and in the overall asymmetrical "press piece" technique of irregular patches stitched together on the backing of the crazy quilt.

While the fad of crazy quilts was overwhelming in many urban centers, more conventional quilts continued to be made in smaller cities and rural sections. Many were presentation quilts. The majority were true quilts, not tufted pieces like most crazy throws. Some were traditional pieced and appliqué quilts; others were embroidered coverlets. Red and white pieces, particularly, enjoyed a surge of popularity during the last decade of the 19th century and the first twenty years of the 20th. Fund-raising quilts of all types were made in great numbers after the Centennial.

102. Detail of piecework sampler quilt, c. 1861, Ohio, Westminster area. Made by Ann Rudy (b. 1841). 80" x 69". Plain and printed cottons. Each of the fifty-six piecework squares is a different design. The double border of green figured fabric does not show. Rose-colored calico borders the pattern blocks.

103. Piecework sampler quilt, d. 1854, Boston, Massachusetts. Maker unknown. 94" x 82". Silk and velvet; silk embroidery. Clearly the work of a skilled seamstress, this quilt presents nearly every pattern available to the piecework quiltmaker. Joining the small bits of silk and velvet used in so many of the blocks must have been a tedious, but rewarding, task.

104. Piecework and appliqué sampler quilt, c. 1880, Edge Grove, Pennsylvania. Maker unknown. 79½" x 78½". Printed and plain cottons. A tan border surrounds blocks pieced in deep red, rose, gray, and gold and set in a pale-blue ground. There is nothing technically difficult about the patterns chosen for this quilt, but the subtle balance and color choices suggest the hand of an experienced maker. This is one of the many quilts whose story would be interesting to know. It may have been fashioned as a visible file for pattern construction, as each pattern is quite different from the others, and some are very complex.

105. Piecework and appliqué sampler quilt, c. 1914, Ohio. Maker unknown. Printed and plain cottons; cotton embroidery. 82" x 74". Red edging surrounds a border of burgundy print on gold. Piecework Bear's Paw, Sawtooth, Chimney Sweep, Wild Goose Chase, and Pine Tree mix with Baskets and a variety of triangle-based piecing. Appliqué squares include an Oak-Leaf Reel, one in cutwork, and a charming dog. The quilt suggests that a Pennsylvania influence was still alive in 20th-century Ohio. A number of squares are signed in embroidered outline stitch and include fabrics of light green and shades of red and gold.

106. *Opposite page:* Piecework and appliqué friendship album quilt, d. 1935, American, possibly Southern. Maker unknown. Printed, check weave, and plain cottons; cotton embroidery. 86" x 74½". In all forty-two blocks of this quilt, few patterns are repeated, but the whole is tied together with pastel Depression-era fabrics, apple-green sashing, and white

corner blocks. Helia Keeran dated her square on Valentine's Day, embroidering "2-14-35". Was this a Valentine gift for a friend? Betty, Donald, Marie, and Russel added House blocks. Mary Martha Heller had a Butterfly memory block dedicated to her by her daughter. Other Keerans, Shavers, and Ackers simply added their names. As is often the case with quilts of this era, stitching seems a little crude. A mixture of needlework skills underlines the combination of given and whole names.

107. Piecework and appliqué sampler coverlet, c. 1885, Vermont. Maker unknown. 72" x 72". Silk, velvet, and machine-embroidered ribbons; silk and cotton embroidery. Repeat use of fabrics and the similarity in pattern orientation suggest a single maker for this sampler. Like most of the block-format "tile" or "crazy" quilts, this piece is not a true quilt. It lacks batting between the layers.

108. *Opposite page:* Piecework and appliqué theme sampler, c. 1925, American, mid-South. Maker unknown. 74" x 64". Plain cottons; cotton embroidery. The maker used dozens of embroidery stitches, but the "Lazy Daisy" was especially pertinent to her theme —"DAISIES wont tell". "ZETTIE", "HOME", and "HE LOVES ME" are among the legends on other squares. What a curious and fascinating naïve coverlet!

Busy Lives and Busy Quilts

Relief from managing the complex Victorian household could be found in fancywork. The crazy quilt, also known as puzzle patchwork, among other names, was women's favorite outlet. Odd scraps of all sorts of fine fabrics like velvet, silk, and satin, were laid in place over a backing. Seams were usually accented with embroidery, and more embroidery decoration, ribbons, and patches were stitched on the irregular base. Well-organized crazy quilts sparkle like jewels with these additions.

109. Piecework and appliqué crazy quilt top, unfinished, c. 1888, American. Maker unknown. 80" x 58". Silks, velvets, and lace; silk embroidery. Unfinished quilt tops provide many clues about crazy quilt construction, but they can rarely answer questions about the purpose of a quilt. Was this top to be a memorial or a friendship quilt? Now it is impossible to tell. The blocks, like those in most fancywork coverlets of the era, were made in the "press piece" manner—each scrap was sewn to a cotton backing. Then the quilt top was assembled, and each block identified by a scrap of paper inscribed with a name. "Mrs A. Cole", "Mrs Frank Whiting", and "Hattie Frankland" are among the women noted. Did they make the blocks? Several squares are tiny pieced pattern constructions. One special block combines four tiny patterns (Basket, Pinwheel, Broken Dishes and Diamond), the embroidered initials "S.S.K.", and the dates "1799" and "1888", suggesting that friends made a memorial for S.S.K. at the latter date.

110. Piecework and appliqué crazy patch slumber throw, c. 1880, American. Maker unknown. 63" x 63". Silks and machine-embroidered ribbons; silk embroidery. No blocks were used to make this "parlor" or "slumber" throw. The entire face is made of odd-shaped scraps, attached like jigsaw puzzle pieces to the backing. Then, the maker, "JK," embroidered the throw, which might easily be termed an album or lexicon of embroidery stitches. In one group of patches, she stitched "Welcome my friends all". Several vignettes of children, inspired by Kate Greenaway's drawings, are scattered throughout. The maker's efforts are put in a somewhat frivolous perspective by an 1883 article on crazy quilts in *The Delineator:* "If its construction is not the sort of work that will aid in making the world greater, it at least is *work,* and that is something good." Happily, such half-hearted enthusiasm did not deter "JK." She finished her work with an elaborate striped border.

111. Detail of a piecework crazy quilt, late 19th century, Brewster, Massachusetts. Made by Almira Lincoln Boggs. 61½" x 58". Silk, velvet, silk ribbon; cotton embroidery and paint. Squares in deep Victorian colors—maroon, deep blue, brown, gold, rust, and black—are embellished with painted and embroidered flowers, butterflies, and stitched figures in the Kate Greenaway style. Minute corner blocks, also decorated, interrupt the pieced sashing. The coverlet is tied, or tufted, with threads instead of quilting. Tufting was much more practical for pieces combining varied textiles worked in the puzzle patchwork style.

112. *(Above),* **113.** *(opposite page).* Piecework and appliqué crazy quilt and pillow shams, late 19th century, upper New York State. Maker unknown. Fig. 112, each 27" x 27"; fig. 113, 92" x 63". Plain and pattern-weave silks; embroidery in various materials. Continued use of individual fabrics and consistency in the exquisite embroidery clearly show the hand of a single maker. Was this set the gift of a doting mother to a child fascinated by the circus? Horseback riders of both sexes prance through most squares, but other circus figures appear, too, particularly the colorful birds and clowns certain to delight a child. Many figures are stuffed to add an extra dimension. A few equestriennes are so finely finished that the lower part of their riding habits or skirts lift to show a daring glimpse of pantaloons.

Like most of the crazy-quilt genre, this set is pieced with a great variety of fine fabrics. Striped taffeta—woven with its pattern— and other taffetas and silks combine in a busy, but carefully orchestrated block-form spread. The competition for design and textile variety in crazy quilts was tremendous. If women could not find handsome scraps at home, they searched far and wide. Dry goods dealers, department stores, and mail-order houses like Montgomery Ward were apparently besieged by requests for fabric samples. The 1894-1895 Ward's catalogue mentioned that the firm's cuts were "in such small pieces as to be useless for fancy or crazy-patch-work." Trading scraps was a common way to increase a hoard. Some women advertised for trades their friends could not provide.

As Penny McMorris points out in her excellent article, "The Crazy Quilt: A Fabric Scrapbook," if scraps were wanted, silk manufacturers quickly obliged. One firm advertised in the March, 1884, *Ladies Home Journal:* "We will mail odds and ends from work rooms— just the thing for 'crazy patchwork.'" The intrigue of scraps was an integral part of the era's values, values promoted by womens' magazines and public opinion. Most women accepted as a credo the responsibility for making a home beautiful. The belief was widespread. One woman in *The Ohio Farmer* newspaper (1883) wrote: "An ugly, unattractive, humdrum home never did produce an aspiring, beautiful soul." How could anyone ignore such appeals?

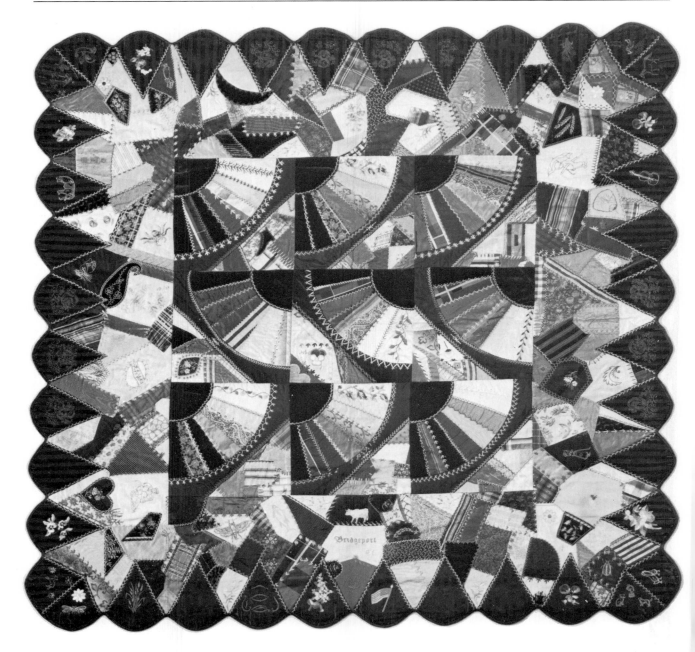

114. Piecework and appliqué crazy quilt, d. 1884, Bridgeport, Connecticut. Made by Martha E. Beach (1840-1921). 54½" x 54¾". Silks, satins, velvets, ribbons, and cottons; cotton embroidery. Fans in the Japanese taste, so popular after 1876, make up the center blocks of a scrapbook album. One patch is labeled "Bridgeport", and some contain embroidered initials ("C.M.B.", "D.C.B.") and the date "1884."

115. *Opposite page:* Piecework and appliqué crazy quilt, third quarter 19th century, Granville, Vermont. Made by a member of the Haskins family. 82" x 69". Printed and plain cottons. Family members and farm animals were captured in appliqué portraits, but the exotic menagerie must have come from a book.

116. Piecework and appliqué crazy botanical album slumber throw, c. 1890, Baltimore, Maryland. Made by Augusta Elizabeth Duvall Bussey (1843-1932). Silk; various embroidery materials. 73" x 73". Augusta Elizabeth Duvall Bussey was a botanist who worked her subjects into an exquisite album. Each of the nine blocks features a different flower or plant, embroidered in the large center patch. Corner patches are similarly embroidered, and more flowers and plants are scattered throughout the crazy patches. A red cockscomb, strawberries, and holly are only three of the specimens chosen for the quilt.

117. *Opposite page:* Piecework and appliqué friendship memory quilt, assembled c. 1905, Minneapolis, Minnesota. Makers: Florence Barton Loring (1847-1925, assembled and contributed to the quilt), Olive Frances Barton (mother of Florence), Mrs. Isaac Atwater, Julia Estes, Mrs. Loren Fletcher and others. 77" x 65". Silks, satins, plain and machine-embroidered ribbons, and printed patches; various embroidery materials. Blocks for this quilt were made at the end of the 19th century in the then-reigning Japanese taste. But that fashion's demand for asymmetry was modified somewhat by the makers. These leaders of Minneapolis society imposed a broaded ribbon grid on their irregular press-piece blocks. This collection of fabrics shows the incredible variety available to wealthy women making crazy patchwork throws. Others found their patches through mail-order and in trades, producing different results. Here, moiré, striped and brocaded silks, velvets, gros de Tours, ikats, and satins—mostly gathered from dressmaking scraps or from treasured, but worn, clothing—are carefully combined.

When the history of a piece is recorded—as this one is—it provides a base for speculation about histories of other women and their work. Florence Barton Loring was an accomplished musician, civic leader, and strong supporter of many societies and charities. She, her friends, and relatives embellished squares to recall their interests. One square features Red Cross nursing; another holds the musical notation of favorite musical themes—the beginning of the last movement of Beethoven's 9th Symphony and the first phrases of Schumann's Quintet. Peacock feathers flourish with pride, horseshoes symbolize good fortune, and homely details, like a teapot and towel, call up the ever-present domestic theme. Family pets are not forgotten. An Egyptian motif is a tribute to the cradle of civilization, while an embroidered American flag and DAR button fly over a fan with the embroidered names of European countries on its leaves. Imagine the makers busily gathered over their handiwork and sharing the concerns they stitched in its squares!

Stitched Quilts: The Embroidered Coverlet

Embroidery stitches, often found in small amounts on album quilts, became an important element in the quilt lexicon of the late 19th century. From their appearance as extensive ornament on crazy patchwork quilts to this final evolution—the sole decoration—was a short transition. By the turn of the century, embroidery patterns similar to today's iron-on transfers were published in magazines and sold singly.

118. *Opposite page:* Embroidered friendship presentation quilt, d. 1899, Louisville, Kentucky. Made by the members of the congregation of St. Charles Church. 108" x 72". Plain cotton; red cotton embroidery. A skillful representation of St. Charles Church is worked in the center of this quilt in whipstitch (now often called outline stitch) and chain stitch. Ladies of the congregation embroidered this gift for the founding priest of St. Charles, Reverend C. P. Raffo, who probably supervised the church construction, done, from the look of the quilt's portrait, about a decade earlier. The frame building with fish-scale slates would then have been the height of fashion. One maker added a legend beneath the building: "St. Charles Church/Louisville, Ky/ Presented to the Rev. C. P. Ruffo/ Lenten Monday, April 3d 1899". "SUSAn WILBER" signed the Cross and "J.J. Gaffney" signed the crescent (at the right) in the center block. "Sacred Heart/ Society" and "Altar Society" are embroidered on the heart and star in the lower corners of the square. Hundreds of other members of the parish are represented on embroidered motifs adapted from piecework quilt patterns and simple geometric forms. Some squares hold names added around concentric hearts, stars, diamonds, and in pinwheel arrays.

Names flare like compass points in four circles and are added to one rococo-style cartouche. The corner blocks each hold four fleurs de lis, Louisville's signet.

119. *Above:* Detail of fig. 120. Long a symbol of romantic love, coy Victorian cherubs link hands in dance between butterflies and birds. Embroidery like this relies on the sentimental trade and greeting cards of the era for its imagery.

120. Embroidered wedding quilt, d. 1895, probably Pennsylvania. Made for Harvey S. and Gallie A. Cope; maker unknown. 71″ x 77″. Plain cotton; red cotton embroidery. It seems that red was the color of choice for the embroidered quilts made in the decades which bracketed the turn of the 19th century. Happily, these reds have not faded. The quilt, with its vignettes of seasonal bliss, is still lively. Most of the scenes could be traced directly to some illustration in a magazine, book, print, or greeting card of the day. Kris Kringle may have stepped right out of *St. Nicholas,* the popular children's periodical. The chubby child in what looks like a Pennsylvania Windsor highchair is, however, an exception—perhaps a wishful suggestion. The curious scene of a sturdy woman with an umbrella might well be a cartoon the maker and the Copes once smiled over together.

121. Embroidered coverlet, d. 1892, Beloit, Ohio. Made by Mary Woolman and friends. 67″ x 69½″. Plain cotton; wool embroidery. When is a "coverlet" a "quilt"? The terms are often confused by the makers themselves. The maker of this unstuffed coverlet—Mary Woolman, herself—calls this a "quilt . . . made in the year of 1892 by fifteen of my young lady friends". The young women were between fifteen and twenty-two years old when they stitched their motifs in the then-prevailing Japanese style. Most embroidery is in whipstitch.

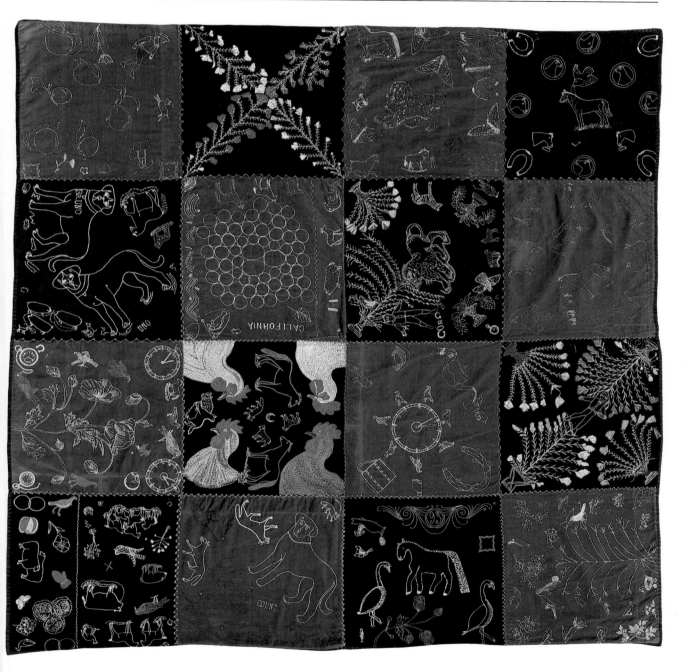

122. Embroidered album quilt, d. 1893, California, Oakland area. Made by the More children (under the supervision of their mother) for their grandmother. 54" x 66". Cotton velvet; cotton embroidery.

An extraordinary family album of mementos, foliage, farm animals, and a wild menagerie was an undoubted Christmas favorite of the family's grandmother. Three boys are embroidered here, perhaps portraits of the three young Mores.

The farm dogs are included, as is a square which shows one dog, "Count", rescuing the livestock from wolves. Worked in whip-stitch, couching, blanket, chain, and feather stitch.

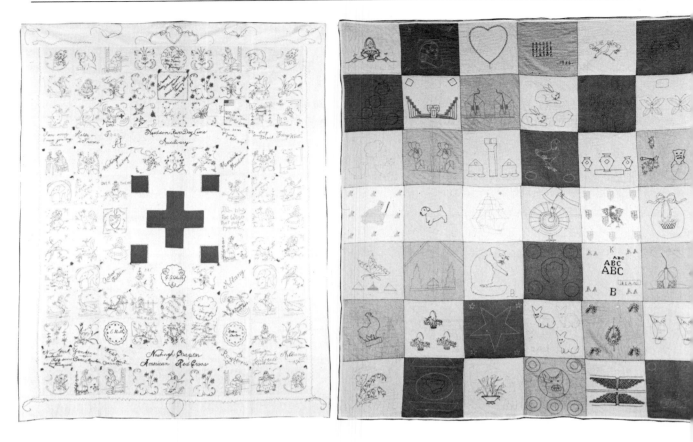

123. Embroidered and appliqué remembrance coverlet, c. 1918, New York, Newburgh area. Apparently made by the members of the Hudson River Day Line Auxiliary, Newburgh Chapter of the American Red Cross. 80½" x 59¼". Plain cotton; red cotton embroidery. Purchased blocks with pre-printed patterns combine with other, more personal, allusions to family, to New York City and upstate communities, and to the Hudson River Day Line—an excursion service which still plies the river today. The central block is an appliquéd Red Cross surrounded by blocks recording the names of the Day Line's boats. Other squares feature the Franco-American alliance and slogans of World War I: "Over There", "Hello France", "The Rose of No Man's Land", among others. At the top is an American flag, embroidered with the verse "If ye break faith/ with us who die,/ We shall not sleep" from "In Flanders Fields" by John McCrae, first published in 1915 and still well-loved.

124. Embroidered coverlet, d. 1936, American. Maker unknown. 79½" x 69". Plain and printed cottons; cotton embroidery. Embroidered coverlets continued to be made through the Depression and are still made today. Here a naïve artist combined printed patterns with others adapted from advertisements of the period. It seems that a single maker fashioned this spread, as stitching is technically similar throughout.

Diversity and Change

Many friendship and presentation quilts of the last decade of the 19th century and first third of the 20th have a graphic quality quite different from earlier pieces. Usually, the patterns were simpler than the old pieced Weathervane, or the basket-, star-, and block-form patterns. Appliqué quilts were also more linear and easily made. During this period, the Schoolhouse quilt appeared and embroidered fan and ray designs developed, but the painless Chimney Sweep continued. Coverlets made of tobacco patches and flour sacks were also fairly popular, perhaps a response to the economy. Embroidery was used more often than ink to mark or sign these later quilts.

125. Pieced friendship quilt, c. 1930, Pennsylvania, Mercer County. Maker unknown. 92½" x 72". Plain cottons; cotton embroidery. Initials and typically Amish names are added.

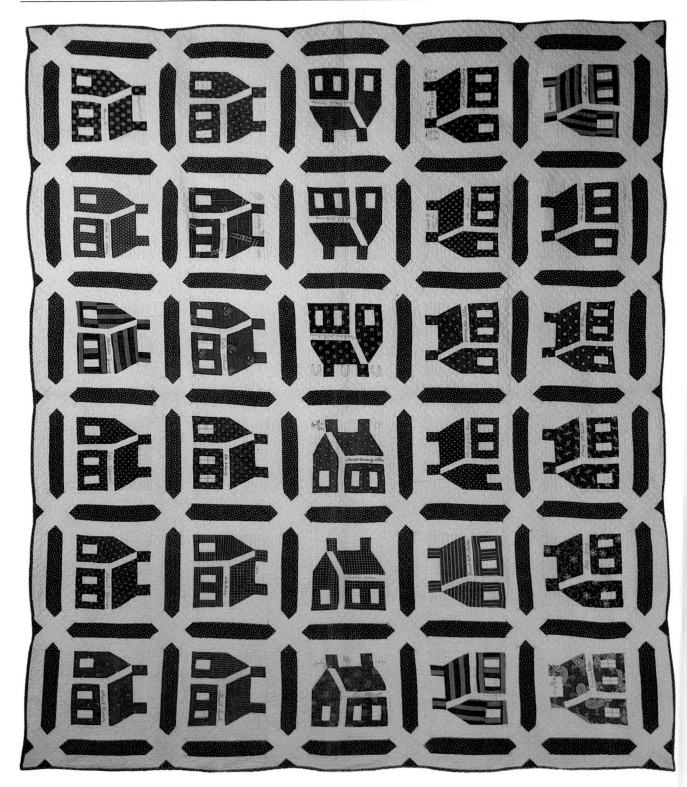

126. *Opposite page:* Appliqué friendship quilt, d. 1890, 1891, 1892, Cincinnati, Ohio. Maker unknown. 76" x 91". Printed and plain cottons; cotton embroidery. Signed "To Mary" in several squares with names of Carney, Dickerson, and Hartman women embroidered in the space between the roof and walls of the houses. Hearts, horseshoes, and leaves were added throughout.

127. *Above:* Appliqué presentation quilt, c. 1890, Ohio. Made by the members of an Ohio Methodist Church. 103¾" x 73". Plain cottons; ink inscriptions. This Compass quilt was a fund-raising project for congregation members, whose signatures indicate a 25¢ donation. The finished piece was presented to Charles H. Stocking, minister.

128. *Right:* Detail of piecework presentation quilt, d. 1891, American. Maker unknown. 85" x 70". Plain cottons; silk embroidery, ink inscriptions. The architectural quality of this quilt is appropriate to the legend embroidered in the center: "Presented to B. J. Harwood by Willing Workers of his Ward/ 1891". Colors here are restricted to red and white.

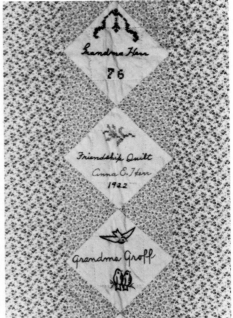

129. *Left top:* Piecework family friendship quilt, d. 1922, Pennsylvania, southern Lancaster County. Made by members of the Herr family. 70" x 62". Printed and plain cottons; cotton embroidery, ink and paint. One square has been painted by one of the family members, but most are embroidered in whipstitch and cross-stitch.

130. *Above:* Detail of fig. 129. The maker chose to title the spread "Friendship Quilt".

131. *Left bottom:* Embroidered presentation quilt, c. 1925-1930, Dane, Wisconsin. Made by church members of Immanuel United Church of Christ. 76" x 92". Plain cotton; cotton embroidery. The quilt was made for Pastor Zenk and his wife, and embroidered signatures of all church members were added before presentation.

132. Piecework presentation quilt, d. 1932. Made by Alice D. Allen for her brother F.E. Corpe. 74" x 67". Printed cottons; ink inscription. Alice Allen labeled her patriotic quilt "July 4, 1932/ F.E. Corpe". It is made of tobacco plug pouches, pieced together with patriotic sashing.

133. Piecework quilt, d. 1935-1936, probably High Point, North Carolina. Makers unknown. 80" x 66". Printed and plain cottons; cotton embroidery. Probably a class project intended as a gift for a favorite teacher, this colorful quilt features Depression-era fabrics in large Chimney Sweep motifs. "High Point School" is stitched on the quilt along with names, including "Chuckey Byerly", "Verdie Lyttle", and "Cora B. Jessee". All point to a North Carolina origin.

The Problem of Money

Helping others has often been women's work and men's money. Fund-raising quilts are good examples of this axiom. For over a century American women have been raising money through subscription quilts. They provided the patterns, the fabrics, and the stitching—but the hard cash was quite often given by men. Women donated pocket money and persuasion. Quilt design has varied with fashion. The earliest one here is a crazy patchwork quilt, but surely others were made long before this. Piecework fans and the embroidered compass-fan were often fund-raisers. The object was to collect the most money in the smallest space. For this, small triangle-based piecework was also very satisfactory. Churches and community groups made the quilts and quite often raffled them to eke out the last possible dollar. Occasionally, the total raised is mentioned on the quilt.

134. Piecework and appliqué fund-raising quilt, d. 1882, Kentucky. Made by several Baptist groups and individual church members. 96" x 96". Silk, satin, velvet; embroidery in various materials. The block format simplified organization of squares from several groups and individual contributors, each of whom gave at least $18 to fund a failing Kentucky Baptist orphans' home. The project raised $5000—far more than the total suggested by the $18 minimum.

135. Embroidered quilt, d. 1898, Grants Pass, Oregon. Maker unknown. 69¼" x 67⅜". Plain cotton; red cotton embroidery. Emblazoned on the top is "GRANTS PASS DIRECTORY 1898". Many directory quilts also served as fund-raisers, but this piece could have been the work of a single proud wife, promoting her husband's position. Each of the pie-shaped segments in the nine circles contains the name of a business. "Hotel Josephine/ J.O. Booth/ prop"; "Lumber and Fruit Boxes/ S.P.D.L. Co."; "Rogue River Courier"; "M. Clemens/ Druggist"; "Wells Fargo Express Co./ V. T. Perkins Agt."; and "Roy Bartlett/ County Clerk" are a few of the listings.

136. Piecework fund-raising quilt, c. 1895, Atlanta, Georgia. Made by Mrs. Margaret Culberson on behalf of the women of the Park Street Methodist Church, Atlanta. 82½" x 74". Plain cottons; ink inscriptions. Jeff Pierce inscribed this red and white quilt with 810 names. The donation amount was 10¢. Many of the prominent citizens of Atlanta, friends, people from outside Atlanta, and even some who lived in neighboring states provided contributions. The quilt was one of several projects needed to pay for a new church building.

137. Piecework quilt, c. 1914, Little York, New Jersey. Made by the Ladies Aid Society of Little York Methodist Episcopal Church. 92″ x 80″. Plain cottons; cotton embroidery. The large number of embroidered signatures—over 450—suggests that this simple bar quilt served to raise revenue for the Ladies Aid Society. Its very basic pattern adds to this conclusion, since most fund-raising quilts are made in the easiest, most efficient manner. Friendship quilts, on the other hand, tend to be more complex. Most have a piecework or appliqué pattern which provides a challenge for the maker. Oddly enough, makers of fund-raising quilts were likely to spend extra time adding signatures in embroidery, not inscribing them in ink. They may have found this effort gained more contributions.

138. Detail of piecework quilt, d. 1908, 1909, 1910, Lima, Ohio. Maker unknown. 84¼″ x 69⅜″. Plain and printed cottons; cotton embroidery. Lima, Ohio's Rebecca Auxiliary met over Hunter's Drug Store and pieced this variant of the Old Maid's Puzzle pattern. Each block has a name and date embroidered, but none indicates that the signer was the maker of the quilt. Ida Warner, O. Schurz, Ella Smith, Netta Sherman, and Laura B. Tinsk were among the signers of 1909. M.S. Coon added "Jan. 1910". Several signed more than one square. It is not possible to determine whether this was a fund-raising or a friendship quilt.

139. Piecework fund-raising quilt, c. 1917, Medford, Oregon. Made by the ladies of the Methodist Episcopal Church South, Medford, Oregon. Plain cottons; cotton embroidery. The favorite colors red and white were again chosen for this fund-raising quilt. Hundreds of names are embroidered including, Mrs. Ida Frisbee, Mrs. M. G. Mordraff, Florence Townsend, Bernice Smith, Morrill Walker, and others. One midwife listed the names of all the children she had helped bring into the world!

140. Appliqué fund-raising quilt, d. 1927, American, possibly Sioux City, Iowa. Made by members of the Aurelias. 88½" x 70". Plain cottons; cotton embroidery. Thirty blue-starred blocks hold 720 names, which appear to have been stitched, in blue, by one or two women. Aurelia High School is well known in Sioux City, Iowa, and titles like "Deputy Superintendent" added to some names suggest the school and city.

141. *Opposite page:* Piecework fund-raising quilt, d. 1919, Indiana, Scotland area. Made by the ladies of the Scotland, Indiana Christian Church. 90" x 78". Silk, satin, and velvet; cotton embroidery. This brilliant crazy patchwork is, in fact, a tied quilt—complete with interlining. Over 500 names are embroidered in every part of the fan design. Curiously, the names include "Spot" and "Bingo," perhaps two generous pets? The church was founded in 1890 and still exists, although the town is no longer in existence.

142. Piecework fund-raising quilt, c. 1922-1932, Kansas City, Missouri. Made by members of Mercy Hospital Club. 72" x 83". Plain cottons; ink inscriptions. Another red and white quilt, pieced this time in an "X and O" pattern, served as a fund-raising project. Names are handwritten in the white spaces. The quilting was machine stitched in a three-leaf clover pattern.

143. Appliqué coverlet, c. 1935, Prescott, Ontario, Canada. Maker unknown, but possibly the women's auxiliary of Amity Lodge, Odd Fellows Lodge No. 80. 89½" x 87". Plain cottons; cotton embroidery. A blue ground with pale gold appliquéd figures was a combination often chosen for fund-raising quilts made after 1930. Most of these have embroidered names, as seen here. This coverlet, though done like a business directory, quite possibly was a revenue quilt. One square contains "F L T [Freedom, Love and Truth]" with three linked circles; "AMITY LODGE -NO. 80- / PRESCOTT-ONT-'' embroidered around a circle with "Mr. James Clint/ Noble Grand" centered inside. Another holds "EMPIRE Tea Store", and nearby is "L. McGillis/ Furniture Dealer".

144. Detail of appliqué fund-raising quilt, d. 1935, 1936-1938, Lima, Ohio. Made by Miss Bertha M. Abbott and embroidered by Miss Luta J. Abbott. 85″ x 82⅜″. Plain and printed cottons; cotton embroidery. A scalloped border encloses three sides of this quilt, appliquéd in a red and gray Schoolhouse pattern. Centered is the legend: "TOWNSEND CLUBS/ NO'S 1 & 2/ DR FRANCIS E. TOWNSEND,/ FOUNDER/ LIMA = 1935 = OHIO". Names of over 420 people are embroidered in fan arrays between the appliqué squares. Most are from Lima, Ohio, but a number of names were added along with hometowns like Yuma, Arizona; New York, New York; Fort Wayne, Indiana; Chicago, Illinois; and many small and large Ohio cities. Ticket sales for the quilt netted $111.60, an impressive sum during the Depression. The Townsend Clubs were a considerable organization during that period.

145. Piecework and appliqué fund-raising quilt, 1984, New Albany, Indiana. Made by the Christian Womens' Fellowship of the Central Christian Church, New Albany, Indiana. Designed by Susan Parrett. 94″ x 94″. Plain and printed cottons. Fund-raising quilts are still being made today. There seems to be a return to more elaborate designs and even to album quilts and samplers, like this one. Raffles of the finished quilt are the most usual source of revenue, for collectors now look for the excellent design and fine needlework which characterize the best of these quilts.

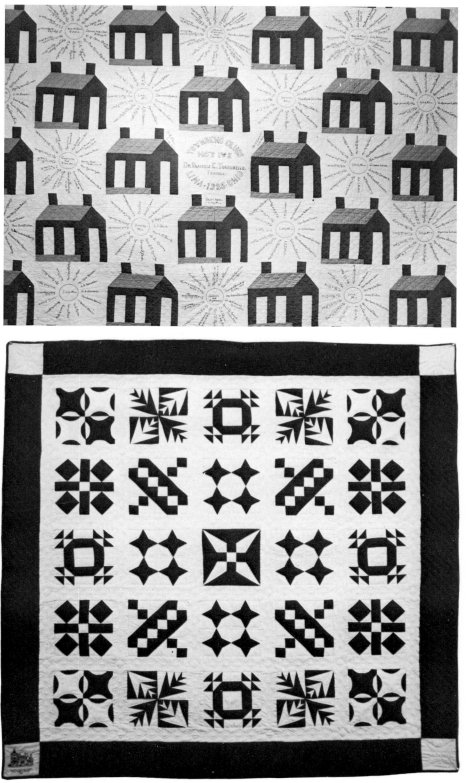

5. "A Tribute of Respect": Contemporary Quilts for America

Women in postwar America faced a changing social climate where quiltmaking played a negligible role. Fortunately, a small number of women throughout the country continued to quilt, keeping the art alive and preserving its required skills for granddaughters and great-nieces who rediscovered crafts in the 1960s. During the 1970s, interest in quilts and other folk arts swelled. Seminal books were published, and museum exhibitions of early bed covers helped develop public awareness. Old quilts inspired new ones.

The Bicentennial celebration of 1976 provided the focus for Americans' renewed interest in their heritage. Thousands made album quilts—done in the same square block format developed more than a century earlier. Museums received countless donations of Bicentennial quilts, while hundreds more were sent to President and Mrs. Gerald R. Ford. Scout troops and elementary school children traveled to Washington, D.C., to deliver their gifts personally—awed as much by their own creativity as the occasion.

If the study of the mundane was unpopular and sometimes ignored in the academic world, all this fascination with heritage, or roots, was infectious. No doubt it prompted more scholars and museums to concentrate on ordinary people and the common products of their daily life, a field difficult to study because records are sparse. As scholars turned to this more intimate, more domestic arena, they found that women had made important contributions, with quiltmaking, of course, one of their long-lived accomplishments. Special studies of early quilts, like The Kentucky Quilt Project, began to record this heritage. Ohio, Texas, Utah, Pennsylvania, California, Missouri, Minnesota, and Michigan are among the many states where similar projects are in various stages of completion.

Today, women everywhere are making quilts in hundreds of forms, album and friendship quilts prominent among them. Women still collect signatures of such notables, past and present, as Grace Kelly, Bing Crosby, and Richard and Pat Nixon for autograph

146. *Opposite page:* Appliqué and piecework Bicentennial album quilt, 1976, Jacksonville, Oregon. Made by the Jacksonville Booster Club. Designed by Ann and Bruce Butte. 94" x 78". Plain, printed, and check-weave cottons and cotton blends; cotton embroidery. Groups throughout the country, like the Jacksonville Booster Club, were galvanized by the Bicentennial to create heritage quilts for their communities.

quilts. Many fund-raising projects feature friendship quilts. In fact, several have been made to raise money for the restoration of the Statue of Liberty. Some of these quilts are revivals of familiar techniques and are usually made in small-figured and plain cottons or cotton blends similar to earlier fabrics. Patterns for old album designs help women create contemporary versions of early models, but many quilters design new blocks to express ideas significant for them right now. Other artists experiment with combinations of traditional and exciting new technology. Many continue to work in the block format. Groups of friends still collaborate on special quilts. One thing is certain—album and friendship quilts will remain in the quilter's repertoire because these quilts say now, as before, "Forget me Not."

147. Piecework presentation quilt, d. 1944, possibly Wisconsin, Racine area. Made by the Grendale Unit #416, American Legion Auxiliary. 86" x 77". Plain cottons; cotton embroidery. Although quiltmaking was not extremely popular just before World War II, the war effort did encourage an occasional special presentation quilt—often tied, as this is, perhaps to save precious time. Most of the 469 women whose names are embroidered here were members of the many union chapters, like "Federation of Labor #401" or "Bell Telephone #427", stitched in the centers of various stars. These groups were significant to the wife of Senator Smith, the apparent recipient. Colors are navy blue, yellow-gold, and white.

148. *Bicentennial Gifts,* a Philadelphia exhibition of remembrances sent to President and Mrs. Gerald R. Ford in 1976, veritably exploded with album and heritage quilts.

149. Piecework and appliqué remembrance album quilt, 1985, Chattanooga, Tennessee. Made by members of the Eastside Branch of Senior Neighbors. 94" x 76". Printed and plain cottons; cotton embroidery. Each contributor added his or her preferences for "My Favorite Things" inside a basket. Most are flowers or fruit, but some are particularly ingenious. Blocks with a pencil, pen, and Eastside stationery; a pair of sewing scissors; a set of cooking tools; the Easter bunny with chick and egg; and one collection of soft drink bottles are set among the traditional tributes of album quilts. Most makers stitched their names somewhere in the blocks.

150. Detail of fig. 149. Bets Ramsey, coordinator, remarks that "Jessie Martin's block was made by her sister, Ruby Beard, to show how Jessie loved to do laundry in her younger days."

151. Appliqué and piecework album quilt, c. 1980, Texas, Kingswood area. Made by the "Quilt Bats." 68" x 80". Plain and printed cottons; cotton embroidery. Group members Gwen Emmett, Dianne Klesstad, Sidney Delaney, Rosalind Cruzan, Kay Hudek, Phoebe Gregory, and Sandra Williams stitched their names on the back of the quilt, entitled "Texas Wildflowers." Each contributed a flower.

152. Detail, center panel of St. Paul's Episcopal Church, Chattanooga, Tennessee, Bicentennial quilt, c. 1976. Panel by Bets Ramsey. The entire quilt is piecework and appliqué in plain and printed cottons with embroidery details.

153. Appliqué album quilt, 1984, Morton Grove, Illinois. Made by Nancy Pearson. 78" x 78". Plain and printed cottons; cotton embroidery. Titled "Nancy's Garden," this contemporary album is designed from a square surviving from a quilt made in 1845. It won two awards at the 1984 South/Southwest Quilt Association exhibit, Houston, Texas.

154. *Above:* Appliqué and piecework remembrance quilt, 1983, Chattanooga, Tennessee. Made by the Senior Neighbors, East Chattanooga Branch, at the Mary Walker Center. 60" x 74". Plain and printed cottons; cotton embroidery. "Childhood Memories," as this quilt is called, began with story-telling, and the vignettes here vividly illustrate these stories. Such recollections as a bad boy getting a switching, making Christmas popcorn balls, making butter, and cooking a stolen piece of ham are given a visual context in a remembrance album.

155. Piecework panel. Made by Catherine Jansen. 25" x 20". Color xerography on cotton. A textile artist educated at Cranbrook Academy of Art and Tyler School of Art, Jansen has spent the last dozen years experimenting in photography and quiltmaking. Combined images are a specialty. In this companion piece to fig. 156, a typed explanation of her quilt's progress was made by color xerography on fabric and pieced with samplings of flower photographs.

156. Piecework garden album quilt, 1984, Wyncote, Pennsylvania. Made by Catherine Jansen. 72" x 48". Color xerography on cotton. Throughout an entire year, Jansen photographed plants blooming in her Wyncote garden. Floral panels are combined with foliage in an exciting interplay of images which recalls the appliqué chintz spreads of the first half of the 19th century. Yet the artist uses today's technology to gain this surprising effect.

157. Machine-quilted bordered view, "Seaside Vacation," 1984, Edgecomb, Maine. Made by Gayle Fraas and Duncan W. Slade. 24″ x 24″. Procion dyes on cotton. Of these "bordered views," Duncan Slade comments in *Maine Today:* "We feel that we are paying homage to traditional quiltmaking in our art," an art which combines detailed painting on pima cotton with some quilted details. Gayle Fraas explains that "the 'views' are not pieced and hand-quilted because that would make them look too soft. We prefer the hard lines of machine quilting, but we do some hand quilting in the landscapes where the detail is too fine for the machine stitch." This piece is somewhat unusual in that it is a photograph album about albums themselves. Many of the Fraas-Slade bordered views contain representations of antique quilts or motifs taken from Oriental rug patterns. Both are used as the borders of elaborate landscapes, interiors, or architectural views.

158. Detail of fig. 153.

Credits

Frontispiece: The Abby Aldrich Rockefeller Folk Art Center, Williamsburg, Va. Gift of Mr. and Mrs. Foster McCarl, Jr. Catalogue 76.609.6.

Introduction: **1.** Courtesy of Independence National Historical Park, Philadelphia, Pa. Gift of Mr. and Mrs. Elliston P. Morris. Catalogue 10361. **2.** Courtesy of the Wadsworth Athenaeum, Hartford, Ct. **3-5.** Ludy Strauss, The Quilt Gallery, Santa Monica, Ca.

Chapter 1: **6.** M. Finkel & Daughter, Philadelphia, Pa. **7.** Courtesy of Shelburne Museum, Shelburne, Vt. Catalogue 10-29. **8.** New York State Historical Association, Cooperstown, N.Y. Gift of Sen. Walter W. Stokes. Catalogue N-222-56. **9.** Philadelphia Museum of Art. Gift of Mrs. Sterett Ridgely Prevost. Accession 1982-134-1. **10-11.** Daughters of the American Revolution Museum, Washington, D.C. Gift of Mrs. C. Edward Murray, Curator General. Catalogue 5254. **12.** Oakland Museum, Oakland, Ca. Gift of Mrs. A.Z. Rimoldi. Catalogue 68.204.2a. **13.** Dr. and Mrs. Donald M. Herr. Photograph by Karin Strawbridge. **14.** Atlanta Historical Society, Atlanta, Ga. Gift of Miss Dorothy Wilson Seago. Catalogue 75-236-1. **15.** Courtesy of Shelburne Museum, Shelburne, Vt. Catalogue 10-151. **16.** Maryland Historical Society, Baltimore. Gift of Miss Mary Bartow Steuart. Catalogue 55.8.1.

Chapter 2: **17.** Collection of Merry Silber. Photograph by Peter Glasser. **18-19.** Daughters of the American Revolution Museum, Washington, D.C. Gift of Mrs. Minna S. Golden. Catalogue 82.130. **20.** From the collection of Mr. and Mrs. Herbert B. Feldmann. Photograph courtesy of Bettie Mintz. **21-22.** Pink House Antiques, New Hope, Pa. Photograph by Peter Glasser. **23.** Philadelphia Museum of Art. Given by Mr. and Mrs. Percival Armitage. Accession 42-4-1. **24.** Daughters of the American Revolution Museum, Washington, D.C. Gift of Mrs. Benjamin Catchings. Catalogue 7124. **25.** Smithsonian Institution, Washington, D.C. Catalogue T.11149. **26.** Maryland Historical Society, Baltimore. Gift of Mrs. Alan D. Chesney. Catalogue 66.79.1. **27.** Maryland Historical Society, Baltimore. Gift of Mrs. Alice F. Hecht. Catalogue 70.56.1. **28.** Collection of Mrs. Herman Greenberg. Photograph courtesy of Bettie Mintz. **29.** Collection of Nancy and Jeffrey Pressman. **30.** Sandra Mitchell, Southfield, Mich. Photograph by Peter Glasser. **31, 34.** Daughters of the American Revolution Museum, Washington, D.C. Gift of Dr. Kate I. Leatherman. Catalogue 7045. **32.** Maryland Historical Society, Baltimore. Gift of Mrs. Milford Nathan. Catalogue 53.36.1. **33.** Stella Rubin, Quilts and Country Antiques, Potomac, Md. **35.** Maryland Historical Society, Baltimore. Gift of Mrs. Frances Marie Smart, Mrs. James Whitaker, and Mrs. Joseph F. Wood. Catalogue 79.29.1. **36.** Philadelphia Museum of Art. Given by the five granddaughters of Samuel Padgett Hancock: Mrs. Levis Lloyd Mann, Mrs. H. Maxwell Langdon, Mrs. George K. Helbert, Mrs. Nelson D. Warwick, Mrs. Granville B. Hopkins. Accession 45-35-1. **37.** Jackie Schneider, Just Us, Tucson, Az. **38.** Shelly Zegart's Quilts, Louisville, Ky. **39.** Ray Featherstone, The Country Shop, Westfield, Ind. **40.** From the collection of David P. and Susan M. Cunningham. **41.** Courtesy of The Brooklyn Museum, Brooklyn, N.Y. Gift of H. Randolph Lever. Accession 71.163. **42.** Collection of Ross Trump, Medina, Ohio. Photograph by Peter Glasser. **43.** Ludy Strauss, The Quilt Gallery, Santa Monica, Ca. **44.** Stella Rubin, Quilts and Country Antiques, Potomac, Md. **45.** Private collection. Photograph courtesy of Susan Parrett and Rod Lich, Folkways, Georgetown, Ind. **46.** Collection of Ross Trump, Medina, Ohio. Photograph by Peter Glasser. **47.** Jackie Schneider, Just Us, Tucson, Az. **48.** Courtesy of Shelburne Museum, Shelburne, Vt. Catalogue 10-38. **49.** Ray Featherstone, The Country Shop, Westfield, Ind. **50.** Judith and James Milne, New York, N.Y. **51.** Private collection. Photograph courtesy of Federation Antiques, Inc., Cincinnati, Ohio. **52.** Atlanta Historical Society. Gift of Mr. and Mrs. Jesse Draper. Catalogue 72-302-2. **53.** Newark Museum, Newark, N.J. Gift of Miss Katharine A. Righter. Accession 61.506. **54.** Newark Museum, Newark, N.J. Purchase 1948 Sophronia Anderson Bequest Fund. Accession 48.1 **55.** Collection of Bettie Mintz, All of Us Americans Folk Art, Bethesda, Md. **56.** Collection of Jones New York at Home, New York, N.Y. Photograph courtesy of Phyllis Haders. **57.** Jackie Schneider, Just Us, Tucson, Az. **58.** Museum of Our National Heritage, Lexington, Mass. Gift of Mrs. Everett C. Carey. Accession 74.1.43. **59.** From the collection of Ellen and Melvin Gordon. Photograph courtesy of Bettie Mintz, All of Us Americans Folk Art, Bethesda, Md. **60.** Sloan Museum. Photograph courtesy of the Folk Arts Division, the Michigan State University Museum, East Lansing, Mich. **61.** Collections of Greenfield Village and the Henry Ford Museum, Dearborn, Mich. Accession 55.136.2.

Chapter 3. **62.** Collection of Bettie Mintz, All of Us Americans Folk Art, Bethesda, Md. **63.** Chester County Historical Society, West Chester, Pa. Gift of Mrs. Helen Wood Shortlidge. Catalogue 34. Photograph by Thomas Landon Davies. **64.** State Historical Society of Wisconsin, Madison. Gift of Mrs. Julia E. Hicks. Catalogue 46.294. **65.** Brooks Antiques, Lahaska, Pa. Photograph by Peter Glasser. **66.** Chester County Historical Society, West Chester, Pa. Gift of Mr. and Mrs. Ellis E. Stern. Catalogue 37. Photograph by Thomas Landon Davies. **67.** Jackie Schneider, Just Us, Tucson, Az. **68.** Jackie Schneider, Just Us, Tucson, Az. Photograph courtesy of M. Finkel & Daughter, Philadelphia, Pa. **69.** Ray Featherstone, The Country Shop, Westfield, Ind. **70.** Courtesy of Shelburne Museum, Shelburne, Vt. Gift of Blanche Esther Field.

Catalogue 10-333. **71.** Chester County Historical Society, West Chester, Pa. Catalogue 47. Photograph by Thomas Landon Davies. **72-73.** Chester County Historical Society, West Chester, Pa. Gift of Mrs. Robert J. Merrick. Catalogue 1981.15. Photographs by Thomas Landon Davies. **74.** Collection of Merry Silber, Birmingham, Mich. **75-76.** Collection of Laura Fisher, Gallery 57, New York, N.Y. **77.** Chester County Historical Society, West Chester, Pa. Gift of Mrs. Leonard W. Coleman for Katie Isabel Hoopes. Catalogue 36. **78.** Sandra Mitchell, Southfield, Mich. Photograph by Peter Glasser. **79.** Newark Museum, Newark, N.J. Gift of Miss Edith C. Wenman, 1958. Catalogue 58.101. *Quilts in the Newark Museum,* pp. 48-50. **80.** Stella Rubin, Quilts and Country Antiques, Potomac, Md. **81.** M. Finkel & Daughter, Philadelphia, Pa. **82.** Abby Aldrich Rockefeller Folk Art Collection, Williamsburg, Va. Catalogue 62.609.1. **83-84.** Chester County Historical Society, West Chester, Pa. Gift of Mrs. Robert H. Davis. Catalogue 133. Photographs by Thomas Landon Davies. **85.** New York State Historical Association, Cooperstown, N.Y. Gift of Thomas Doubleday. Catalogue N-120.73. **86.** Collection of Laura Fisher, Gallery 57, New York, N.Y. **87.** Wisconsin State Historical Society, Madison. Gift of Mrs. Virginia Senn Brown. Catalogue 1970.237. **88-89.** Daughters of the American Revolution Museum, Washington, D.C. Gift of J. Frederick Cain. Accession 84.11. **90-93.** Collection of Merry Silber, Birmingham, Mich. **94.** Southern Oregon Historical Society, Jacksonville, Ore. Gift of Mrs. M.H. Beale. Accession 61.126.2. **95.** The State Historical Society of Wisconsin, Madison. Gift of Mr. and Mrs. Leslie R. Morris. Catalogue 1976.132.1. **96,98.** Owned by Pat Nickols. **97,99.** Ray Featherstone, The Country Shop, Westfield, Ind. **100.** Jay Johnson Inc., American Folk Heritage Gallery, New York, N.Y.

Chapter 4: **101.** Photograph courtesy of Jackie Schneider, Just Us, Tucson, Az. **102.** From the collections of the Allen County Historical Society, Lima, Ohio. Gift of Mrs. Fred (Laura Rudy) Biteman, the niece of the maker. Catalogue 1053.2. **103.** Reproduced with the permission of Phyllis George Brown, Louisville, Ky. **104.** Stella Rubin, Quilts and Country Antiques, Potomac, Md. **105.** Judith and James Milne, New York, N.Y. **106.** Collection of Laura Fisher, Gallery 57, New York, N.Y. **107.** Private collection. **108.** Collection of Shelly Zegart, Shelly Zegart's Quilts, Louisville, Ky. **109.** Collection of Laura Fisher, Gallery 57, New York, N.Y. **110.** Smithsonian Institution, Washington, D.C. Catalogue T.11233. **111.** Daughters of the American Revolution Museum, Washington, D.C. Gift of Jeannette O. Baylies. Accession 76.112. **112-113.** The Clokeys, Pleasant Valley, N.Y. **114.** Kansas City Museum, Kansas City, Mo. Catalogue 72.970. **115.** Courtesy of Shelburne Museum, Shelburne, Vt. Catalogue 10-215. **116.** Smithsonian Institution, Washington, D.C. Catalogue T.13517. **117.** Minneapolis Institute of Art, Minneapolis, Minn. Gift of Eleanor Atwater, Martha Atwater, Sandra Butler, Willie Connovan, Suzanne H. Hodder, Anita Kunin, Laura Miles, Eleanor W. Reid, and Katherine Scott. Accession 82.139. **118.** Collection of Elaine Sloan Hart. Photograph courtesy of The Kentucky Quilt Project, Inc. **119-120.** Ludy Strauss, The Quilt Gallery, Santa Monica, Ca. **121.** Collection of Merry Silber, Birmingham, Mich. **122.** Oakland Museum, Oakland, Ca. Catalogue 70.32.1. **123.** Collection of Laura Fisher, Gallery 57, New York, N.Y. **124.** Sandra Mitchell, Southfield, Mich. Photograph by Peter Glasser. **125.** Collection of Laura Fisher, Gallery 57, New York, N.Y. **126.** Sandra Mitchell, Southfield, Mich. Photograph by Peter Glasser. **127.** Smithsonian Institution, Washington, D.C. Catalogue T.13892. **128.** State Historical Society of Wisconsin, Madison. Catalogue 1974.1.35. **129-130.** Collection of Dr. and Mrs. Donald M. Herr. **131.** State Historical Society of Wisconsin, Madison. Gift of Immanuel United Church of Christ. Catalogue 1979.233.1. **132.** Southern Oregon Historical Society, Jacksonville, Ore. Gift of Mrs. Margorie Nicolson. Accession 68.102. **133.** Collection of Laura Fisher, Gallery 57, New York, N.Y. **134.** Collection of the Kentucky Baptist Homes for Children. Photograph courtesy of the Kentucky Quilt Project, Inc. **135.** Southern Oregon Historical Society, Jacksonville, Ore. Gift of Harold David Carr. Catalogue 77.95.1 **136.** Atlanta Historical Society, Atlanta, Ga. Gift of Adair McCarley Woodall. Catalogue 78-13. **137.** Tewksbury Antiques, Oldwick, N.J. **138.** From the collections of the Allen County Historical Society, Lima, Ohio. Gift of Lena Schnabel Snyder. Catalogue 1480.5. **139.** Southern Oregon Historical Society, Jacksonville, Ore. Gift of Mrs. Don Benedict. Catalogue 81.99.1. **140.** Collection of Laura Fisher, Gallery 57, New York, N.Y. **141.** Ray Featherstone, The Country Shop, Westfield, Ind. **142.** Kansas City Museum, Kansas City, Mo. Gift of Mr. and Mrs. Frank Pelletier. Catalogue 72.1021. **143.** Sandra Mitchell, Southfield, Mich. Photograph by Peter Glasser. **144.** From the collections of the Allen County Historical Society, Lima, Ohio. Gift of Miss Bertha Abbott. Catalogue 616.36. **145.** From the collection of Ruth and Maurice Parrett. Photograph courtesy of Folkways, Georgetown, Ind.

Chapter 5: **146.** Southern Oregon Historical Society, Jacksonville, Ore. Gift of the Jacksonville Booster Club. Catalogue 78.136. **147.** Sabra Petersman, Peace & Plenty, Los Angeles, Ca. **148.** *Bicentennial Gifts,* 1977, First Bank of the United States. Photograph by Richard Frear, National Park Service, courtesy of Independence National Historical Park, Philadelphia, Pa. This is a small portion of the collection of the Gerald R. Ford Museum National Archives and Record Service, Grand Rapids, Mich. **149-150.** Eastside Branch of Senior Neighbors. Photographs by John Coniglio, courtesy of Bets Ramsey. **151.** Collection of the "Quilt Bats," Kingswood, Tx. Photograph courtesy of Kay Hudek. **152.** Collection of St. Paul's Episcopal Church, Chattanooga, Tenn. Photograph courtesy of Bets Ramsey. **153.** Photograph courtesy of Nancy Pearson. **154.** Collection of the Senior Neighbors, 10th & Newby Center, Chattanooga, Tenn. Photograph by Ronald Farmer, courtesy of Bets Ramsey. **155-156.** Catherine Jansen, Wyncote, Pa. Artist's photograph. **157.** Gayle Fraas/ Duncan Slade. Courtesy of The Works Gallery, Contemporary Art, Philadelphia, Pa., Ruth Snyderman, Director. **158.** Photograph courtesy of Nancy Pearson.

Bibliography

Berry, Michael W. "Documenting the 19th-Century Quilt." *American Craft* 45 (February/March 1985): 23-27.

Carlisle, Lilian Baker. *Pieced Work and Appliqué Quilts at Shelburne Museum.* Shelburne, Vt.: The Shelburne Museum, 1957.

Curtis, Philip H. *American Quilts in the Newark Museum Collection.* Newark, N.J.: The Newark Museum Association, 1974.

Dunton, William R., Jr. *Old Quilts.* Catonsville, Md.: privately printed, 1946.

Finley, Ruth E. *Old Patchwork Quilts and the Women Who Made Them.* Newton Centre, Mass., 1929; rpt. Watertown, Mass.: Charles T. Branford Co., 1971.

Frye, L. Thomas, ed. *American Quilts: A Handmade Legacy.* Oakland, Cal.: The Oakland Museum, 1981.

Haders, Phyllis. *The Main Street Pocket Guide to Quilts.* Pittstown, N.J.: The Main Street Press, 1983.

Hall, Carrie A. and Rose C. Kretsinger. *The Romance of the Patchwork Quilt in America.* New York, 1935; rpt. New York: Bonanza Books, n.d.

Holstein, Jonathan. *Kentucky Quilts, 1800-1900.* Louisville: Kentucky Quilt Project, 1982; rpt. New York: Pantheon Books, 1983.

——. *The Pieced Quilt: An American Design Tradition.* Greenwich, Conn.: New York Graphic Society, 1973.

Ickis, Marguerite. *The Standard Book of Quilt-Making and Collecting.* New York: Dover Publishers, Inc., 1949.

Katzenberg, Dena S. *Baltimore Album Quilts.* Baltimore: The Baltimore Museum of Art, 1981.

——. *The Great American Cover-Up: Counterpanes of the Eighteenth and Nineteenth Centuries.* Baltimore: The Baltimore Museum of Art, 1981.

McMorris, Penny. "The Crazy Quilt: A Fabric Scrapbook." *Art & Antiques* (September-October, 1983).

Montgomery, Florence M. *Printed Textiles: English and American Cottons and Linens 1700-1850.* New York: The Viking Press, Inc., 1970.

"One Sews, The Other Doesn't." *Down East: The Magazine of Maine;* rpt. 1984 annual *Maine Today;* 70-72, 104, 105.

Orlovsky, Patsy and Myron. *Quilts in America.* New York: McGraw-Hill Book Co., 1974.

Percival, Maciver. *The Chintz Book.* London: William Heinemann, Ltd., 1923.

Peterman, Sabra. "Album Quilts: A Glimpse into Our Past," in *Los Angeles Antiques Show.* Los Angeles: Junior League of Los Angeles, Inc., 1981: 35-42.

Peto, Florence. *American Quilts and Coverlets.* New York: Chanticleer Press, 1949.

Robinson, Charlotte, ed. *The Artist & the Quilt.* New York: Alfred A. Knopf, 1983.

Safford, Carleton L. and Robert Bishop. *America's Quilts and Coverlets.* New York: E.P. Dutton & Co., 1972.

Swann, Susan Burrows. *Plain & Fancy: American Women and Their Needlework, 1700-1850.* New York: Holt, Rinehart and Winston, 1977.

Verey, Rosemary. *The Scented Garden.* New York: Van Nostrand Reinhold Company, 1981.